I RISE UP

A Journey to Self-Love and Empowerment

HANNA OLIVAS

ALONG WITH 14 INSPIRING AUTHORS

ISBN: 978-1-968061-74-6

TABLE OF CONTENTS

INTRODUCTION

There comes a moment in every woman's life when she realizes she can no longer stay where she is. Maybe it's the weight of heartbreak, the sting of rejection, or the quiet ache of never feeling "enough." Maybe it's the moment she looks in the mirror and barely recognizes herself—or the moment she decides to finally choose herself, once and for all.

I Rise Up was born from those moments.

This book is for every woman who has been knocked down by life but found the courage to stand again. It is for the ones who have been silenced, overlooked, or underestimated—and still chose to rise. It is for you.

Within these pages, you'll find real stories, deep reflections, and practical steps to help you heal what's broken, reclaim what's been lost, and rediscover the powerful, radiant woman within you. This journey is not about perfection—it's about progress, permission, and power. It's about learning to love yourself without apology and stepping into your life with boldness, beauty, and truth.

You don't have to walk this path alone. Let this book be your companion and your guide. As you rise, know this: your story matters. Your healing matters. Your voice matters.

And most of all—**you matter**.

Let's begin.

Hanna Olivas

Founder and CEO of SHE RISES STUDIOS

https://www.linkedin.com/company/she-rises-studios/
https://www.facebook.com/sherisesstudios
https://www.instagram.com/sherisesstudios_llc/
www.SheRisesStudios.com

Author, Speaker, and Founder. Hanna was born and raised in Las Vegas, Nevada, and has paved her way to becoming one of the most influential women of 2022. Hanna is the co-founder of She Rises Studios and the founder of the Brave & Beautiful Blood Cancer Foundation. Her journey started in 2017 when she was first diagnosed with Multiple Myeloma, an incurable blood cancer. Now more than ever, her focus is to empower other women to become leaders because The Future is Female. She is currently traveling and speaking publicly to women to educate them on entrepreneurship, leadership, and owning the female power within.

I Rise Up

By Hanna Olivas

I never planned on being this woman. I didn't grow up thinking I'd be the face of resilience or strength. In fact, there were more days I felt like I was barely breathing than days I felt powerful. Life handed me pain before it handed me peace. It carved out holes in my heart before I even knew how to love myself.

But somehow, through all of it, I learned to rise.

And I want to talk about that. Not the highlight reel. Not the curated version of strength you see online. I'm talking about the rising that happens when no one is watching. When the room is silent and your soul is screaming. When you're exhausted and broken and still manage to whisper, "Not today. I'm not done."

That's what I mean when I say, "I rise up."

I've been through hell and back more times than I can count. Not figuratively. Literally. Childhood trauma. Abuse. Loss. Sickness. Watching my body betray me and still having to get up and lead. My story is not a fairy tale. It's not glamorous. It's real. It's full of wounds, war zones, and whispered prayers I wasn't sure God even heard.

But I'm still here. And that alone is a miracle.

There were moments I didn't want to rise. Let's be real. I wanted to stay down. I wanted to disappear. I wanted the noise to stop. But the thing about rising is, it isn't about being fearless. It's about rising even when you're terrified. It's about getting up even when everything in you is screaming to stay small.

There were mornings when I woke up and thought, *I can't do this*. And then, I did it anyway.

Not because I'm some kind of superwoman. But because something deep inside me wouldn't let me give up. Because my daughters were watching. Because the women around me needed someone to go first. Because my pain had a purpose and I refused to die with it locked inside me.

You see, rising up doesn't mean you have it all figured out. It means you choose faith over fear. It means you keep going even when your legs are shaking and your voice is cracking and your heart feels like it's breaking all over again.

It means you let your scars speak louder than your silence.

I've had days where I was running multi-million-dollar projects and moments later crying in the bathroom because I felt like I was drowning. That's real. That's me. That's what being a woman in this world often looks like. Carrying the weight of everyone and everything and still smiling. Still serving. Still standing.

But here's what I learned. You can't rise if you keep pretending you're fine when you're not. You can't rise if you keep stuffing it all down and hoping no one notices. You have to face the parts of you that are still bleeding. You have to look at your reflection and say, "I love you even here. Even in the mess."

That's the start of the rising. Self-love in the middle of the ashes.

I had to learn to love myself when I was unrecognizable. After diagnosis. After heartbreak. After betrayal. After I had nothing left to prove. That kind of love doesn't come from the world. It comes from the fire. It's forged in moments when you think you're alone, but God is whispering, "Keep going. I'm not done with you yet."

And so, I rose. Not just once. Again and again. Every time I got knocked down. Every time someone said I couldn't. Every time I was told I was too loud or too broken or too complicated or too much.

I rose up with faith. With tears. With stubborn hope.

And let me be clear. I still rise up.

Even today. This very day. I still have to remind myself that I am worthy. That I am strong. That I am not defined by what tried to destroy me. I still fight for my peace. For my joy. For my healing. For my family. For my dreams.

Because rising is not a one-time event. It's a decision you make over and over and over again.

There's a woman reading this right now who thinks she's too far gone. Too messed up. Too stuck. And I want to say this to you.

You are not done. You are not broken beyond repair. You are not too late.

You are a warrior. You are a woman who has been through storms and still has breath in her lungs and fire in her bones. You are made of more than the pain. You are made of purpose.

But you have to rise.

Even if you're scared. Especially if you're scared.

You rise by taking one small step. Maybe that step is saying no for the first time. Maybe it's leaving a relationship that's been dimming your light. Maybe it's finally starting the business or writing the book or applying for the thing you've been too afraid to dream about.

You rise by remembering who the hell you are. Not what they told you. Not what life tried to strip away. Who you really are underneath all of it.

You rise with faith. With grit. With grace.

And no, it won't be easy. But it will be worth it.

Because every time you rise, you give another woman permission to do the same. Every time you speak your truth, you break chains.

Every time you choose to stand, even with trembling legs, you become a lighthouse for someone else lost at sea.

You don't have to be perfect. You just have to be brave.

I'm not the same woman I was ten years ago. Or five. Or even one. Because every season I go through shapes me. Some stripped me down to my soul. Others built me back up. But all of them taught me this: I am not here to stay quiet. I am not here to shrink.

I am here to rise and rise and rise until the day I take my last breath.

And I hope you'll rise with me.

Because this world doesn't need more perfect women. It needs more real ones. More raw. More resilient. More powerful women who know how to walk through the fire and come out glowing. It needs you.

So cry. Yell. Rest. Rage. Pray. Heal.

And then, rise.

Every time you rise, you rewrite your story.

You are not what happened to you.

You are what you choose to do next.

And I pray, with all the love and fire in my heart, that you choose to rise.

For you.

For the girl you used to be.

For the woman you're becoming.

For the daughters watching you.

For the women standing behind you.

For the future only you can build.

I rise up because I have no other choice. Because staying stuck is no longer an option. Because my life matters. Because my voice matters. Because my legacy will not be built on fear but forged in fire.

And so will yours.

Let them feel your rise.

Let it shake the ground beneath you.

Let it wake the part of you that's been sleeping for too long.

Let it echo across generations.

You are the storm. You are the sun after the rain. You are the chapter someone else needs to read so they don't give up.

You are the reason I know it's possible.

You are the proof that rising is not a myth.

You are the movement.

So get up.

Stand tall.

Speak loud.

And rise.

You were never meant to play small.

You were meant to rise.

And I'll be rising right beside you.

Always.

Rachael Britton

Breaking Limitations Coaching
Licensed Psychologist & Business Coach

https://www.linkedin.com/in/rachael-britton-05641763
https://www.facebook.com/BreakingLimitationsCoaching
https://www.instagram.com/breakinglimitationscoaching
https://www.breaking-limitations.com/courses
https://www.breaking-limitations.com/consultation

Dr. Rachael Britton is a Licensed Clinical Psychologist, business coach, and educator who helps women redefine success by aligning with their strengths instead of pushing against their wiring. With nearly two decades of experience in mental health, Rachael specializes in trauma-informed care, navigating barriers to growth, and empowerment-based coaching. She is the founder of Breaking Limitations, a platform that supports high-achieving, big-hearted women who feel stuck, scattered, or burned out from trying to meet everyone else's expectations. Through her writing, workshops, and programs, Rachael blends clinical insight with personal truth, helping others shift from perfectionism and self-doubt to clarity, confidence, and self-trust. Her work is rooted in the belief that healing happens when we stop fixing ourselves and start honoring who we are. Whether through therapy, speaking, or writing, Rachael creates space for women to rise moving from surviving to thriving on their own terms.

From Adversity to Empowerment: My Journey of Growth and Self-Love

By Rachael Britton

Have you ever trusted someone, maybe a teacher, a mentor, or someone in a position of power, only to realize they didn't see you the way you saw yourself?

You thought they'd champion your growth... but instead, they highlighted your flaws.

You believed they understood your heart... but their words made you question your worth.

Their feedback echoed longer than it should have, and not in a good way.

If you've ever been labeled in a way that stuck, even when you *knew* it didn't tell your whole story, then you already understand the beginning of mine.

Long before high school, I carried a quiet self-doubt. A sense that something about me just didn't fit. I'd heard it in the passing comments from other kids, and sometimes more directly to my face. I felt it in how adults responded when I was too energetic, too distracted, too "all over the place." Their words may not have been meant to wound, but they did.

Still, it wasn't until one moment in high school that those doubts found a voice I couldn't ignore.

I had asked a teacher I trusted to write a letter of recommendation for me, someone I thought saw my strengths. I imagined his words would highlight the things I was proud of: my creativity, my drive, my heart, but when I read the letter, my stomach dropped.

"Rachael tends to start things but does not finish them."

Those words didn't just hurt, they struck something tender I hadn't yet been able to name. At the time, I didn't know I was living with undiagnosed ADHD. I didn't realize that my brain was constantly buzzing with ideas and possibilities, making follow-through a challenge not from carelessness, but because I was wired differently.

All I knew was that someone I respected had confirmed my deepest fear: *Maybe I wasn't capable. Maybe I'd never follow through. Maybe I wasn't enough.*

That letter could have broken me, and for a while, it almost did.

When Feedback Feels Like Failure

It wasn't the last time I heard feedback that cut deep. In grad school, the critiques followed me like a shadow:

"A for conceptualization, C for writing. B overall."
*"I just don't think you're emotionally intelligent enough
to be a therapist."*

Each comment felt like proof that maybe I didn't belong in the field I loved. I was working constantly, juggling coursework, bartending, and side hustles, but what others saw didn't match what I knew I was capable of.

One of the hardest moments came when I vulnerably asked a professor for help after missing a deadline. Instead of support, I was met with ego and intimidation. He told me he'd fail me unless I sat in his office and named every one of my shortcomings. I was expected to apologize, flatter his teaching, and admit all the ways I was "falling short" just to avoid being kicked out of the program.

At the time, I didn't realize how unethical that was, and I later learned he was dismissed for mistreating other students, too, but the damage was done. That experience etched in me the belief: *You're broken. You're not enough. You'll never finish what you start.*

Finding Mentors Who Saw More

Thankfully, not everyone treated me that way. I eventually found mentors who didn't just *tolerate* my differences; they *valued* them. They saw my ability to dream big, connect dots, and think expansively not as flaws, but strengths.

They helped me channel that big-picture thinking into manageable steps. They taught me how to build structure without clipping my wings, and they reminded me consistently that my worth wasn't tied to perfection.

Their support helped me realize something I had never fully understood: while some people's expectations reflect *their* needs, there are others who will see and celebrate *you*. They don't want to change you; they want to see you shine.

Their belief in me was the mirror I didn't know I needed, and for the first time... I began to believe it, too.

Thriving... and Still Struggling

Eventually, I earned my doctorate in Clinical Psychology. I built a private practice, launched coaching programs, and started a family. On the outside, I was thriving, and in many ways, I was.

But inside? The old voices crept back in.

You start things but don't finish them.

The busier I became, the more I felt like I was juggling everything but holding onto nothing. I was doing *all* the things, coaching, parenting, building, nurturing, and yet I constantly felt behind. Comments like "You seem scattered" or "You're not really present" hit right at the shame I thought I had already outgrown.

So, I did what I now teach others to do: I got curious.

Owning My Brain, Embracing My Power

I revisited the traits I had been taught to see as flaws and began to see them as clues. What if I didn't have to "fix" myself to fit a mold that was never designed for me? What if I worked *with* my brain instead of against it?

That shift changed everything.

I learned to delegate. I stopped trying to become the detail-oriented planner I'm not and embraced my role as a visionary. I built a team that helped bring my ideas to life. I surrounded myself with people who didn't shrink me, but helped me stay grounded.

Over time, I redefined what "finishing" actually means to me.

Sometimes, finishing looks like checking something off a list, but sometimes, it means letting go of something that no longer fits my values. It might mean walking away from a partnership, pivoting from a plan, or closing a chapter that served its purpose. I stopped equating endings with failure and started seeing them as *completions*.

Turning Pain Into Purpose

Every experience, every stop, start, and stumble, led me to my true calling: helping women like me.

I now work with therapists, coaches, and mompreneurs who are brilliant, big-hearted, and exhausted. Women who have a million ideas but don't know where to begin. Women who love deeply and dream big, but feel like they're falling short, not because they lack drive, but because the world wasn't built for their rhythm, neurodiversity, or gifts.

I help them build systems that support *them*. I teach that success isn't about checking every box; it's about alignment, trust, and honoring your pace. I show them how to rest, how to pivot, and how to rise without shame.

Most of all, I remind them that *failing isn't the same as failure*. It's your **F**irst **A**ttempt **I**n **L**earning (F.A.I.L.). Every time you try, even if it doesn't go as planned, you're gathering new information, building insight, and getting closer to your own goals on your own terms.

Redefining Success on My Terms

My journey isn't linear; it's full of restarts, reevaluations, and reimagining. Luckily, every step brought me closer to who I'm meant to be.

I've learned to lead with strategy, mind, *and* heart. I've learned to define success not by productivity, but by presence, alignment, and joy. I'm no longer just someone who "starts things."

Instead, I'm a creator. A catalyst. A space-holder for transformation.

And now, I want that for you, too.

Your Next Chapter Starts Now

If this story feels familiar, if you've ever felt like you're too much, not enough, or like you just can't catch up, I want you to know:

You are not alone.

You don't need to change who you are to succeed.

You just need the right support and a mindset that honors your wiring, not punishes it.

You're allowed to be unfinished and still be worthy.

You're allowed to try again.

You're allowed to grow on your own terms.

Your next chapter isn't waiting for perfection, it's waiting for *you* to say:

"I'm ready."

And when you are, I'll be here to walk beside you.

Let's take the next step together:
www.breaking-limitations.com/courses

Sonia Rodrigues

Transition to Wellness
Psychotherapist & Coach

https://www.linkedin.com/in/sonia-rodrigues-48b87149/
https://www.facebook.com/SoniaRodriguesLPC/
https://instagram.com/transition.to.wellness
www.transitiontowellness.com
https://soniarodrigues-marto.tribesites.com/

Sonia Rodrigues has been a licensed psychotherapist for over 20 years. She is the owner of a psychotherapy and coaching practice called Transition to Wellness. She has worked with people of all ages, helping them navigate various challenges in their life. She utilizes a holistic approach and provides a safe and supportive environment where her clients can feel supported on their path towards healing from their traumatic experiences and guided towards creating the life they desire. She provides individual therapy, coaching and also offers a variety of workshops on topics related to trauma, post-traumatic growth and fostering resilience.

Rising in My Worth:
From Unseen to Valued and Empowered

By Sonia Rodrigues

I didn't know what was worse, feeling unloved or feeling unseen by someone I loved with my whole heart.

There was a time in my life when I felt like I was doing everything right—showing up, communicating, trying to be honest, compassionate, patient. But no matter how gently or clearly I tried to express what I needed, it was like I was speaking a language he didn't want to learn. He would look through me, change the subject, or retreat into silence. I was left carrying the weight of the conversation, the conflict, and eventually, the relationship itself.

It was confusing at first. Then, it became painful. And finally, it started to make me question my worth.

When you're in a relationship where your voice echoes back at you as emptiness, you start to internalize that silence. I began wondering, *Am I asking for too much? Am I too emotional? Too needy?* That spiral of self-doubt almost convinced me that my desire to feel heard, valued, and respected was unreasonable.

But deep down, I knew that wasn't true. I wasn't asking for grand gestures or perfection. I was asking to be acknowledged. I was asking for my boundaries to matter. I was asking for someone to care when I said, "That hurt me."

What I eventually came to understand was this: Some people withdraw emotionally not because they don't care, but because they don't know how to stay present when things feel uncomfortable. They shut down as a way of protecting themselves. But that withdrawal—their silence, their lack of response—it doesn't feel protective to the one on the receiving end. It feels like abandonment. It feels like erasure.

And for a long time, I met that pattern with anger. I raised my voice when I felt dismissed. I pushed harder when I felt ignored. I wanted him to feel the urgency of my pain. But no amount of anger could draw out someone who was committed to staying hidden.

What began to shift everything was when I started speaking not from my rage, but from my sadness. From my truth. From the raw ache of what it felt like to be emotionally alone in a relationship. And from there, I began a different kind of journey—one that had nothing to do with changing him and everything to do with coming back home to myself.

I started by asking the hard questions. *What am I really feeling beneath the anger? What do I need that I've been too afraid to claim? What does it mean to truly value myself and what I need?*

When I stripped away the frustration, I found deep sadness. I felt rejected, ignored, and confused. But beneath that sadness, I found something else, too, a fierce longing to understand why I was continuing to allow this to happen.

I began turning inward. I stopped chasing validation from someone who couldn't give it, and I began reconnecting with myself. I started journaling to better understand what I was feeling and what my heart was trying to say. I let myself feel everything without judgment—the grief, the disappointment, the guilt of staying too long in a space that no longer nurtured me. I mourned what could have been, but also began to accept the truth of what was.

To heal, I created small daily rituals that brought me back to myself. I walked often, sometimes ran along the beach, letting my body move the pain out of me. I focused on healing not only emotionally, but also physically and spiritually. I lit candles in the evenings and sat quietly with tea and music that made me feel held. I traveled when I could or imagined where I would go next, dreaming with purpose. There is something incredibly healing about new surroundings, fresh air, and the reminder that the world is still full of beauty—even after heartbreak.

I started dancing again. I moved freely, not for performance but for joy. I took myself on solo dates, bought flowers just for me, and wore things that made me feel radiant. I began to treat myself the way I had always wished someone else would. I made space for myself in my own life.

And slowly, I began to rise.

I reconnected with people who saw me clearly, friends who listened with empathy, who sat with my pain without rushing it away. I deepened relationships that honored mutual respect, care, and vulnerability. In doing so, I remembered what it felt like to be valued for exactly who I am.

The Power of Boundaries: Teaching People How to Treat You

Part of reclaiming my worth meant redefining what I would and would not allow. For so long, I tolerated the bare minimum. I made excuses, hoping things would get better. But I reached a point where I realized that continuing to accept poor treatment was an act of self-betrayal. If I wanted love rooted in honesty, respect, and care, I needed to start by setting the standard myself.

Boundaries became the way I protected my peace, not pushed people away. They became a bridge between my self-worth and the relationships I allowed into my life. I no longer stayed silent when something felt hurtful. I spoke up, not with blame, but with clarity. "This is how I need to be spoken to." "This is what I need to feel safe."

"I will not tolerate disrespect or dishonesty." These statements weren't threats—they were affirmations. I was finally honoring the parts of me that had been dismissed for too long.

And what I learned is this: People either rise to meet your boundaries or reveal why they can't. Either way, it's clarity. Either way, you win.

The Need to Be Met with Empathy, Not Dismissal

Another essential part of healing was acknowledging my need to have my emotions met with empathy—not indifference. I had spent too much time explaining my pain only to be told I was overreacting, or that I was "too sensitive." That kind of dismissal leaves you emotionally starving. It's a subtle form of gaslighting that makes you question your reality.

We all deserve relationships where our feelings are held with care. Where someone pauses and says, "I hear you." "That matters to me." "I'm sorry you felt that way—how can I support you better?" Those words aren't complicated, but they are powerful. They tell you: "I see you. I care enough to stay present."

Being met with empathy heals in ways that defensiveness never can. And while I cannot force that kind of emotional maturity from anyone, I can decide not to stay where it's absent. I can choose people who are emotionally available, who don't shame me for having needs, who meet my vulnerability with grace instead of judgment.

The Path Towards Healing

Healing, I discovered, isn't about getting over something. It's about moving through it—gently, honestly, intentionally. It's about speaking your truth even when it feels risky. It's choosing not to settle for relationships that require you to abandon your self-worth. It's realizing that your value was never tied to whether someone else could see it—it was always yours to claim.

There are still days when old wounds resurface. When I remember the version of myself who kept trying to be heard. When I think about how much I craved tenderness and connection and was met with distance. But now, I let those memories rise without shame. I sit with them, breathe through them, and remind myself of this simple truth: *You cannot make someone love you differently. You cannot force someone to grow. You cannot heal someone who refuses to see the impact of their absence.*

I no longer believe I'm too much. I no longer shrink to fit into spaces that can't hold the fullness of who I am. I no longer wait to be chosen, seen, or validated. I choose myself, fully, unapologetically, and with love.

Being seen, heard, and valued begins within. The world often mirrors what we first offer to ourselves. When I started honoring my own voice, others began to listen differently. When I treated my boundaries as sacred, I noticed who respected them and those who didn't.

So, if you're reading this and you feel invisible, silenced, or dismissed, I want you to know: You are not alone. This moment, this ache in your chest, is not the end of your story. It is the beginning of your return to yourself.

You deserve more. You deserve to feel safe, heard, and emotionally held. Your feelings are not too much. Your pain is valid. Your truth is sacred. Don't let anyone minimize what you know to be true or shame you for wanting connection, empathy, and accountability.

And if someone continues to stonewall you, gaslight you, or ignore your needs, know that you have every right to walk away. You're not walking away from love. You're walking toward *self*-love. Toward peace. Toward a life where your light isn't dimmed but honored.

In your healing, look for the small joys. Nourish yourself. Rebuild your spirit. Surround yourself with people who mirror back your strength, not your insecurities. Make room for new relationships, romantic or otherwise—that lift you, support you, and meet you where you are.

You are not too much. You never were. You are enough...just as you are. Your voice, your boundaries, and your needs matter deeply.

You are worthy of being seen. Of being heard. Of being cherished. And even if someone failed to give that to you before, *you* can give it to yourself now.

This is what rising in your worth looks like.

It begins the moment you realize you don't need to earn love—you just have to love and embrace yourself, and the right person will love you! Just keep rising above!

Journal Prompts: To Support Your Rising Up

1. When was the first time I remember feeling unseen or unheard in a relationship? What did I need in that moment that I didn't receive?
2. What are three things I need in order to feel emotionally safe and valued in a relationship?
3. How do I respond when I feel emotionally abandoned? How can I respond differently, with compassion for myself?
4. What old beliefs about my worth am I ready to release?
5. What small acts of love can I give to myself this week to remind me that I matter?

Carmen Maendel

Nate's Property Maintenance LLC
Co-Owner/Business Office Manager

https://www.linkedin.com/in/carmen-maendel-17510944/
https://www.facebook.com/ncmaendel
https://www.instagram.com/maendelcarmen/
http://natespropertymaintenance.com

Hello I'm Carmen Maendel. Nate and I are a husband and wife team. Our fifteen year old son, Josh officially works for our company as well. We have embarked upon an entrepreneurial journey together that is extremely rewarding for all of us. We own and operate Nate's Property Maintenance LLC together. I handle the business on the home front while my husband coordinates our projects on the job sites with our clients and team of workers. We compliment each other very well working together, and remain very service oriented in our company. Some of the business roles I perform are the following: balancing our books, regularly posting to social media, scheduling our clients, arranging purchase contracts for new business equipment, keeping our business licenses and registration up to date, documenting client files, and much more. Nate works with our clients by coordinating all the projects and equipment on the job sites and carefully plans for each of our projects we do down to the finest of details. Nate, Josh, and Carmen

With the Breastplate of Righteousness

By Carmen Maendel

Introduction: Child of God

Hello friend, I am Carmen Maendel, and I am a child of God, a mother, and a wife. I came to the Lord at the early age of thirteen; however, I rededicated my life to Christ as an adult on November 4, 2006. This does not mean that I am perfect or have not had adversity in my life. Quite the opposite, I would say. Some of the negative incidents in my life happen when I am seeking the Lord wholeheartedly. In the book, *I Rise Up: A Journey to Self-Love and Empowerment*, I share my chapter, "With the Breastplate of Righteousness," with stories to help illustrate some of the adversity and challenges I have overcome in life. I hope and pray that these can be an encouragement to you in your own life journey as well.

My Story: The Downward Spiral

My story begins as I moved away to college, and for the first time, I was free to make whatever decisions I wanted with my life. Some of them were good and honorable, and others were not. My father was battling cancer, and someone I loved very dearly died in a car accident during my second year of college. This was a very difficult time for me, and I started some incredibly bad habits when it came to my health. I would stay up long hours writing papers and completing projects, and the vending machine became my "best friend" at that time. I was not getting the exercise I needed and was falling into a deeper pit when it came to believing in myself and having self-confidence in who I was and what I was doing with my life. I changed my major from pre-med to art and business, and I was still very unclear about what my future would look like. I continued on this downward spiral, and it affected every relationship in my life.

I struggled with having a good relationship with my parents, my siblings, my friends, and my boyfriend in college at that time. I felt numb and like I was just floating through life and not appreciating or valuing anything in my life at that time. It was not until I had graduated from that first college that I began to put my life back together again. I thought it was me doing this; however, in retrospect, I realize that God had never taken His hand off my life even before I knew who He was. He had protected me in so many different situations that I could have really gotten myself into trouble, and the Holy Spirit continues to guide and direct me today. On November 4, 2006, I rededicated my life to Jesus, and things began to get better in my life. I was able to drop the fifty pounds I had gained in college and have been able to maintain that same level of fitness up until today. I created a plan for myself that I also used to help encourage and walk alongside my clients, to lose weight and feel better about themselves.

My Plan: Fitness and Nutrition Combined with Self-Love and Empowerment

I started working out daily in the gym or running outside, and paid attention to what I was eating. I cut out snacks, pizza, fast food, and junk food from my life entirely. I began healthy habits, which became my lifestyle to this day. Did you know that if you do something 21 days in a row and then 90 days after that, it can become a habit (a routine of behavior that is repeated regularly and tends to occur subconsciously) and part of your lifestyle—**21/90 Rule.** After spending the summer in England, France, and Spain, I realized that the Europeans were on to something when I came to eat and exercise daily. While I was in Spain, we had a small breakfast of fruit, meat, cheese, and bread. The lunch was the main meal of the day and consisted of a heavy dose of protein and carbohydrates. Dinner was very late, about 9 p.m., preceded by tapas or hors d'oeuvres a little earlier in the evening. Dinner usually was a small sandwich with meat and cheese. I loved their idea of eating a larger meal in the middle of the day instead of the evening, so they had time to burn it off during the day. Today, I incorporated a large salad for my meal in the middle of the day. I add meat and almonds to a mixed salad with carbohydrates, fats, and protein already. I usually have a smaller breakfast and dinner, incorporating all the food groups, in order to maintain a healthy lifestyle.

The **80/20 Rule** is something I have incorporated into my lifestyle as well. Eighty percent of the time, I pay attention to exercise and eating healthy, and twenty percent of the time, I take a break from all of it and enjoy a cheat meal from time to time. Just remember this: "Always follow a cheat meal with a healthy one," and you can get back on track fairly easily. One part of my twenty percent every day is two pieces of dark chocolate. This helps me from building up a craving for chocolate over a period of time. I have always believed in routines and systems as they help keep me organized and moving in the right direction during the day. I usually get up at 5:50 a.m. every day, except on weekends. The weekends are part of my twenty percent. I have a cereal bar with my vitamins and a green smoothie before my workout. I go down the stairs to our gym, where I have my workout clothes already laid out for me. I change and begin either a Strength Training, HIIT Cardio, or Core workout for about thirty to forty-five minutes each day. I spend this time in the gym praying for my friends, family, and church family. After coming upstairs from my workout, the first thing I do is have devotions for about thirty minutes. This time with God is necessary, and if I miss it in the morning, I definitely feel it throughout the day. I then move into a routine of getting dressed and ready for my day. I have specific systems and procedures in place daily for opening and closing our books, checking and zeroing out email, balancing our business account and filing receipts, and checking for leads. This is a quick snapshot of my daily routine.

As I reached my own goals and helped my Maendel Fitness clients, I developed three goals in the areas of fitness and nutrition. I used **SMART Goals** (Specific, Measurable, Attainable, Realistic, Timed) to set various goals for myself and clients. For instance, a **Fitness Goal:** I will do a HIIT workout on the treadmill for thirty minutes every Monday, Wednesday, and Friday for the next six months with 100% accuracy. An example of a **Nutrition Goal:** I will incorporate one large salad into my diet every day for the next six months with 100% accuracy. I recited these goals three times out loud, and encouraged my clients to do the same, in the morning and evening on a daily basis.

I will share a secret with you that I found out about myself. Changing your lifestyle for the better has more to do with discipline than motivation. If you are motivated to do something, then you will stick to it when you feel like doing it. However, if you have the discipline to do something, you will do it regardless of whether you feel like doing it or not. "I would argue that it is not motivation alone that helps you achieve your goals; discipline plays a very large role as well!"— Carmen Maendel, ISSA CFT, CNS, PN1. While intrinsic/extrinsic motivation is built into your DNA, discipline is something that you can learn to do through continuous practice. Forming good habits and being disciplined lead to feeling motivated; a huge transformation can then take place in your life. A mindset shift can and will take place. You will begin to change your negative thoughts into positive ones. An example of this may be the following: "I don't like to be challenged" changed to "I want to challenge myself." Our greatest weakness lies in giving up. The most certain way to succeed in life is to always try just one more time!

Sometimes, you need to break through *limiting factors* (anything that is keeping you from achieving your goals) to believe that you are capable of doing something. You are responsible for yourself. The only one to limit your growth is you. You are the only one who can influence your success. Your life changes when you break through your limiting beliefs. You are in control of a large percentage of your life by the choices you make. You can not control what happens to you; however, you can control how you react to it. Ten percent is what happens to you in life, and 90 percent is how you react to it or your *attitude* about it. Are you going to keep allowing that person— *you*—to hold you back? We can choose how we respond to adversity in our lives. We can either let it break us down, or we can stand up to it and learn from it. We can respond in a way that limits us, or in a more productive way that potentially opens other windows of opportunity to us. I have learned that life is full of ups and downs and wins and losses. Adversity is a large part of this experience and can either be seen as a stumbling block or a stepping stone, depending on how you react to it. Adversity does not have to be a negative thing. You have the freedom to choose how you respond. You will encounter wins, losses, victories, and setbacks during life and your fitness journey; embrace them as they are all part of your fitness experience.

Examples of Possible Limiting Factors

- Wishful thinking vs. doing the hard work
- Setting goals with an unrealistic time frame
- Lack of planning or having systems in place to track your progress
- Lack of commitment or discipline
- Lack of perseverance or sustainability
- My bone structure is too big
- I am not an athletic person
- This is way too hard for me
- I can't lose weight
- I have zero desire to go to the gym
- Some people have won the genetic lottery, and I have not

- It is impossible for me to stay in shape after reaching a certain age
- The only way I can lose weight is to stop eating altogether
- It's a genetic thing for me
- It is just my fate to be like this
- If I am ever able to lose weight, I will just get it right back
- It's too expensive for me to stay in shape
- It takes too much of my time
- Diet programs are too complicated for me to follow
- Carbohydrates make me fat
- I must have an insulin-resistant problem
- It's not that important to me to be in top physical shape
- I don't like healthy foods
- I can't afford healthy foods
- I have a large body frame

Now that we've got that out of our system, **LET'S GET TO WORK!**

5 Steps to Overcome Limiting Factors

1. Establish a solid foundation for your goals instead of "wishful thinking"
2. Set an urgent but realistic time frame to accomplish these goals
3. Set yourself up for success with proper systems in place and tracking devices to monitor your progress
4. Establish your "why." When your confidence lessens, you can remind yourself why you are strongly committed to your goals
5. Set yourself up for success with a plan of consistent sustainability once you hit your goals, so you can maintain your progress for a lifetime

I have also adopted an idea from Dean Graziosi that I want to leave you with about the **7 Layers of "Why."** The way this works is you ask yourself seven layers deep why you are doing something in your life. An example of this is the following: 1) **Why am I passionate about health and fitness?** Because I like to have more energy for the things I love in life, 2) **Why do I like to have more energy for the things I love in life?** Because then I have more quality time with our family, 3) **Why do I want to have more quality time with our family?** Because this brings more unity to our family, 4) **Why is more unity in our family important?** Because we have more peace and quality of life together, 5) **Why is it important to have more peace and quality of life together?** Because honoring your father and mother is biblical and the right thing to do, 6) **Why is honoring your father and mother important?** Because when our son honors his dad and me, he is also honoring God, 7) **Why is it important to honor God?** Because we are made in His image for the specific purpose of honoring, worshiping, and praising Him. This is my seven levels of "why."

"Wishing you the very best in all your
future endeavors, Beautiful!"

Natalie Horseman

Horseman Publishing
MSN, RN, CNOR

https://www.instagram.com/thefamilyremixguide
https://nataliehorseman.com

Natalie Horseman, is a dedicated nurse with nearly two decades of experience in child and family development. Her extensive background in healthcare has equipped her with a profound understanding of resilience and strength. Throughout her career, Natalie has been committed to guiding individuals through life's most challenging moments with both compassion and empathy. Her personal journey of overcoming adversity has deeply fueled her passion for empowering others. Through her writing, Natalie combines practical advice with heartfelt encouragement, creating a sense of community for those navigating life's storms. She believes that while our experiences shape us, they do not define us. Through her contributions, Natalie strives to inspire readers to embrace their inner strength and resilience, offering reassurance that they are never alone on their journey.

Coming Home

By Natalie Horseman

One of the greatest battles I've faced has been learning to feel at home in my own skin. For years, I carried an invisible weight—shame and judgment about my appearance that consumed me from the inside out. Mirrors were my enemy, reflecting a version of myself I couldn't bear to acknowledge. Every glance felt like an accusation, a reminder of how deeply I despised the way I looked. I couldn't shake the belief that no one could ever find me beautiful—especially not myself.

This struggle went far beyond vanity—it shaped how I moved through the world and determined how I measured my worth.

I tried to hide. I wrapped myself in layers, avoided situations that might expose me, and shrank from social connection. I was terrified of being seen—truly seen—because I feared others would judge me just as harshly as I judged myself. Shame became my constant companion, an invisible cloak that weighed me down. I was convinced the world viewed me through the same distorted lens I used on myself.

The Turning Point

It wasn't a dramatic moment, but a quiet breaking point—one ordinary day, worn down by years of self-criticism and isolation. I caught my reflection in the mirror. Normally, I would've looked away. But something made me pause.

For the first time, I saw more than just my physical form. I saw pain—the kind etched into your face when you've carried a heavy burden for too long. The weight of self-hatred. The exhaustion of pretending. The grief of hiding from your own life.

"What would it be like," I whispered to myself, "to stop being my own worst enemy?"

That single question cracked something open. It didn't spark an overnight transformation—healing is never linear. But it marked the start of something new: a shift toward no longer fighting my body, but learning to feel more neutral about it.

Peeling Back the Shame

Healing meant peeling back the layers of shame, one by one. It meant sitting with discomfort instead of pushing it away. And no, I'm not all the way there—I still have days when self-acceptance feels just out of reach. But I've learned to approach my body with less judgment, to see it not as a collection of flaws but as a testament to strength and survival.

I've come to understand that beauty isn't a single standard—it's a spectrum. A mosaic of everything that makes us uniquely ourselves. I started questioning the harsh lens I used and realized: Others don't see me the way I see myself.

Therapy helped me unlearn old beliefs. Slowly, I began to recognize the resilience of my body. It has carried me through grief, heartbreak, joy, and growth. It has endured and adapted, even when I offered it nothing but disdain. My worth is not defined by my shape, my scars, or the number on the scale. It's defined by my strength, my compassion, and the woman I've become.

I am not my imperfections.
I am the woman who has survived them.

Creating a New Reflection

In healing, I've shattered the cruel image I once held and created something new: a beautiful, chaotic, evolving reflection that is wholly mine. Not perfect. But real. And whole.

This journey isn't finished—some days, self-acceptance still slips through my fingers. But with each step, I learn to treat my body not as a burden but as a sacred part of me—worthy of love, kindness, and care.

True self-acceptance doesn't begin with how we look. It begins with who we believe we are.

A Letter to the Woman in the Mirror

To the woman reading these words, maybe seeing your own struggle in mine: You are not alone.

So many of us fight this battle with our reflection, often silently. We've been taught—by society, media, even the people closest to us—that our worth is tied to appearance, that we must look a certain way to be valued.

But what if you gave yourself permission to see through a softer lens? What if, just for today, you looked in the mirror and honored what's reflected—not the so-called flaws, but the strength, the endurance, the quiet bravery?

Your body is a storyteller.
Those stretch marks? Chapters of growth.
That scar? A tale of healing.
The lines by your eyes? Proof of laughter, sunshine, and a life deeply lived.

Practical Steps Toward Self-Acceptance

Self-acceptance isn't a one-time decision—it's a series of quiet, consistent choices that lead you home to yourself. These are the practices that helped me begin that journey. They're not magic solutions, but gentle tools to help you shift the way you see yourself—day by day.

1. Start a gratitude practice for your body.

Each morning or evening, pause and thank your body for something it has done for you. Not for how it looks—but for what it allows you to experience. Maybe it got you through a tough workday, cradled your child in your arms, or simply let you breathe through a moment of anxiety.

This practice helps you shift from critique to connection. It reminds you that your body isn't the enemy—it's your partner. A living, breathing vessel that shows up for you even when you don't always show up for it. And over time, this simple ritual plants seeds of respect that can bloom into love.

Affirmation to try: "I honor my body for all it does for me. I am grateful for its strength, resilience, and the life it allows me to live."

2. Challenge negative self-talk.

We are often our harshest critics. That internal voice can be relentless—commenting on your weight, your wrinkles, your worth. But here's the truth: not every thought is true, and not every thought deserves your belief.

> *When you hear that voice, pause and ask:*
> *"Would I say this to someone I love?"*
> *If not, it's time to rewrite the script.*

Talk to yourself with the same warmth you'd offer a friend. Replace "I'm so disgusting" with "I'm struggling today, but I still deserve kindness." Speak to yourself like you matter—because you do. Healing starts with how we talk to ourselves in the quiet moments.

Affirmation to try: "I am learning to speak gently to myself. I don't have to be perfect to be worthy."

3. Curate your media.

So much of our self-image is shaped by what we consume. Social media, ads, magazines—they often promote narrow, unrealistic beauty standards that leave us feeling unworthy.

Take your power back. Unfollow accounts that trigger comparison or shame. Instead, fill your feed with diverse bodies, stories of healing, and people who radiate authenticity. Seek out creators who celebrate real beauty—not filtered perfection.

When you change what you see, you change what you believe is possible. Representation matters. Let your digital space reflect your values, not your insecurities.

Try this: Do a "feed detox" this week. Ask yourself: "Does this account inspire me—or diminish me?" Choose accordingly.

4. Practice being seen.

So many of us learn to shrink—to hide behind oversized clothes, turned shoulders, or constant apologies. Reclaiming your right to be seen is a radical act of self-acceptance.

Start small. Wear the bold lipstick. Take off the cardigan. Stand a little taller. Post the photo without obsessing over angles. Say yes to being in the picture instead of taking it.

These acts may feel scary at first. But each time you allow yourself to show up without hiding, you prove to yourself that you're worthy of taking up space—just as you are.

Affirmation to try: "I am allowed to be seen. I am allowed to be here, fully and unapologetically."

5. Find your people.

Healing thrives in safe, supportive spaces. Surround yourself with people who love you for your heart, not your waistline. People who lift you up when your inner critic gets loud. People who celebrate your growth, your joy, your messy, miraculous journey.

Let go of relationships rooted in comparison, competition, or criticism. You don't need to earn belonging by shrinking yourself. The right people will never ask you to.

If you don't have that circle yet, seek it out—whether online, in support groups, or through new communities. We were never meant to heal alone.

Reminder: You deserve connection that feels like home. Don't settle for less.

Self-Acceptance Is a Practice—Not a Destination

It's okay if some days feel harder than others. What matters is showing up for yourself with patience and compassion. The small choices you make each day—the kind words, the bold outfit, the unfollow button—add up. They become the foundation for a new way of being.

> *One where you don't just tolerate yourself,*
> *You honor yourself.*
> *One where you don't just survive in your skin,*
> *You thrive in it.*
>
> *You are not too much. You are not broken. You are becoming.*
> *And that is a beautiful thing.*

Rising Together

When I began treating myself with compassion, my whole world shifted. I found my voice. I chased dreams I once deemed impossible. I built deeper relationships—because I was no longer hiding behind shame.

And the most beautiful part? The ripple effect. When I began speaking my truth, other women began sharing theirs. We created space for vulnerability, for healing. We lifted each other.

That's how we rise. Not alone, but together.

By breaking the cycles of shame in our own lives, we give others permission to do the same. We become part of a collective healing—

one that defies the systems that taught us to hate ourselves in the first place.

You deserve to feel safe and whole in your own skin. You deserve joy, rest, celebration, and love—just as you are.

Your body is not an apology.
It is your home.
It is your history.
It is your power.

So, as you take your own steps toward self-acceptance, remember: Progress isn't measured by perfection. It's found in the small wins—catching a cruel thought before it lands, standing a little taller, meeting your own eyes with grace.

This road won't always be easy, but I promise you: The freedom on the other side is worth the fight.

And in that freedom, you will discover something extraordinary.

You've been enough all along.

Rise up, beautiful soul. The world needs your light.

A Note from Natalie –

Self-doubt loves isolation. Don't give it that power.

I'm here to support your journey, counter doubt's lies with truth, and celebrate every brave step you take. Connect with me—let's prove to doubt that it picked the wrong woman to mess with.

Nataliehorseman.com

Lori Ellen Miller

Soul Journey Secrets, LLC
Creator of Soul Cartography™

https://www.facebook.com/share/1FvVHfYC1i/
https://allmebydesign.com/

Lori Ellen Miller is a Spiritual Empowerment Pathfinder and the creator of Soul Cartography™, a transformative system that guides spiritually aware women to stop pushing, proving, or people-pleasing—and start living from the truth of who they are. She helps women with a calling finally understand the patterns, pressure, and emotional weight that have kept them stuck, scattered, or questioning their worth. Through intuitive guidance and deep energetic mapping, Lori walks women home to themselves—so they can rise with clarity, confidence, and compassion. Her work helps them stop chasing and start creating a life of sacred service, aligned with what their Calling and what their Soul actually came here to do.

When Forgiveness Set Me Free:
A Return to Self-Love and Liberation

By Lori Ellen Miller

"We are not what happened to us.
We are what we choose to do with it."

There was a time in my life when I believed life was a series of events that I was a victim of. I thought that things happened "to me" and I just had to accept it, move on, and there was nothing I could do about it. I didn't think about how all of that affected my current life—except that it carried a throughline of unworthiness. A quiet belief that maybe life could never be what I had once hoped it would be.

The traumatic chapter that once defined my childhood had ended decades ago. I had gotten away, physically left that environment, and built what looked like a good life. I poured myself into spiritual growth, personal development, healing modalities, and sacred rituals. On the outside, I was thriving. On the inside, I thought I had healed. But underneath all of that evolution, something still lived in the shadows.

I didn't realize that I was still tethered to the pain. That my body stored the memories in a bank of victimhood and despair.

It had woven itself quietly into my relationships, my sense of self-worth, my finances, and even how I received joy—if I allowed myself to receive it at all. It whispered in the background of my accomplishments: "You have to work harder," "You're not quite enough," "Don't get too comfortable."

If you've ever wondered why healing feels incomplete even after doing "all the work," you're not alone.

That subtle but persistent sense that no matter how far you've come, some part of the past still has a say in your present.

I didn't think of myself as someone who held onto what had happened. I believed I had moved on from it. I had spoken the words. I had done the therapy. But when I truly began to examine the deeper patterns—how easily I could be triggered, how certain interactions sent me spiraling into self-doubt or defensiveness—I had to be honest with myself:

I hadn't really let go.

I began to delve deeper into my soul—exploring the path I had chosen long before this lifetime. I came to embrace that all of it, even the pain, was part of a divine agreement. My soul knew I had everything I needed to come through to the other side as a woman who could spread universal love and what that means for us to live into who we truly are and who we are here to be and express in the world.

Forgiveness was the beginning. And I've learned—it's not always one grand moment of release. It's a layered unraveling. A choice that we sometimes make again and again. And the truth is, I wasn't choosing it. Not fully. Part of me was still gripping the wound like a shield—afraid that if I set it down, I'd lose something. Maybe protection. Maybe justice. Maybe control.

But in holding on, I wasn't protecting myself—I was imprisoning myself.

Forgiveness is one of the most misunderstood aspects of healing. It's not a moral obligation. It's not about excusing harm or letting someone "off the hook." It's not for the person who hurt you—it's for you. It's about reclaiming your energy from a story that no longer defines you.

It's a radical act of self-love.

One morning during a meditative reflection, I received a quiet but clear nudge:

Write the letter.

Not for closure. Not for confrontation. Not to rehash or reframe. Just as a sacred release. A declaration of sovereignty.

And so I did.

I poured my heart onto the page. I didn't filter. I didn't try to be wise or evolved or poetic. I just wrote. Not from anger or blame—but from truth. From the part of me that no longer carried the weight. The tears were a release from what was once so overpowering. In writing, I remembered things I hadn't in years—moments of fun within the darkness, slivers of joy from a childhood that had often felt overshadowed. The letter wasn't accusatory. It didn't point fingers. It was honest. Sacred. Freeing.

I didn't plan to send it. In fact, I thought I'd burn it or bury it, as a ritual of letting go.

But when I finished, I felt a stillness. Then another nudge:

Send it.

And this time, I listened.

I mailed the letter with a strange sense of peace. I didn't know what, if anything, would come of it. But something inside me already felt different. Lighter. Less tangled. The energy inside me was already softer. The story that had been running silently in the background had quieted. I had chosen myself over my pain. I stopped waiting for something outside of me to set me free. I realized it didn't even matter if I received a response.

Weeks later, an envelope arrived.

My hands trembled slightly as I opened it. Inside was a handwritten note. Simple. Unpolished. Raw.

"Thank you. You gave me my life by turning me in," it read. *"I didn't want to do what I was doing, but I didn't know how to stop."*

That line cracked something open in me. It wasn't an apology. It wasn't validation. And in that moment, I saw what I hadn't been able to see before: pain moves in cycles. It repeats itself in those who don't know how to heal it. And while I never excused the harm, I could now recognize the deeper truth—that I had a choice in whether I continued carrying it.

I saw the person behind the pain. Not to justify, but to witness. To truly feel and understand a deeper level of compassion that was greater than myself. To know it in a spiritual sense. He was never able to move through his own childhood trauma. I was able to see that through the years, he had been seeking and searching, but never surrendered to it fully. He couldn't escape what had happened to him—or what he had done to others. He was caught in the cycle of pain, trapped in a darkness so deep he couldn't see the light of his own soul.

And maybe that's what forgiveness really is—witnessing the pain for what it is, and choosing to set yourself free from its grip.

I had been so afraid that forgiving would mean giving away my power. But the moment I truly forgave, I realized I had never been more powerful.

Forgiveness didn't make me weak. It made me clear. Whole. Sovereign.

And it changed how I saw myself. Not as someone broken or wounded—but as someone deeply courageous. Someone worthy of peace, of joy, of love that doesn't need to be earned.

That choice to forgive didn't erase what happened. It didn't rewrite the past. But it reclaimed my present. And it reimagined my future.

It changed how I walked into rooms. It changed how I treated my own heart. It changed how I allowed myself to be loved.

And maybe you're here because something inside you is ready for that shift, too.

You don't have to wait for the apology that may never come. You don't have to wait for someone else to change or see what they did. You don't even have to know how to start.

You just need to be willing to ask: *What am I still carrying that isn't mine to hold anymore?*

What am I ready to release—not for them, but for me?

Forgiveness cracked the door open. Self-love walked me through it.

And that's the journey I want you to know is possible—not because it's easy, but because it's yours to choose. You don't have to be stuck in the cycle. You don't have to keep revisiting the pain just to prove how strong you are.

Your strength is already known. Your courage has already spoken.

The next step is choosing to be free.

I once thought I was stuck. But I was simply waiting. Waiting for readiness. Waiting for the breath of clarity that whispers, "It's time now."

And maybe, right now, that whisper is for you.

Rising up doesn't mean forgetting. It doesn't mean pretending. It means standing in the power of who you are today—choosing peace over pain, choosing self-love over self-protection, choosing your future over your fear.

We are not what happened to us.

We are what we choose to do with it.

Forgiveness set me free.

Self-love taught me how to stay free.

And now, every step I take is a reminder:

> The power to rise has always lived within me.
> And it lives within you, too.

J.J. Mathieu

Author & Astrologer

https://www.facebook.com/jjmathieuauthor
https://www.instagram.com/j.j.mathieu/

J.J. Mathieu is a writer, astrologer and full-time mom with a background in corporate and academic Communication. She earned a Master's Degree in Communication Studies from the University of Rhode Island and is a graduate of Debra Silverman's School of Applied Astrology. J.J. has been writing in a variety of contexts since she was a child crafting fiction books with pencil and spiral-bound notebook in hand. She has worn many hats during her career, but all have centered around or have been influenced by her love of writing. J.J.'s work has appeared on The Barre Blog and MomsIntoFitness.com. Her personal challenges serve as the foundation of her writing, which focuses on inspiring others to see their own lives through a lens of deep compassion and love for themselves and others. In addition to writing, J.J. loves reading, baking, mindful movement and anything chocolate and sparkly. Connect with J.J. at jjmathieuauthor@gmail.com.

So Much to Be Thankful For

By J.J. Mathieu

AUGUST 2010

After a few years of enjoying our freedom as newlyweds, my husband, Taylor, and I knew that we were more than ready to start our family. We took one last vacation to California in January of 2008 and decided that we would throw caution to the wind and see where it took us. I got pregnant in February, only to lose the baby to an early miscarriage at five weeks. Needless to say, I was devastated. However, we decided to try again, and I got pregnant for a second time the very next month. The pregnancy was going along rather smoothly until my 18-week ultrasound at the end of July, when we found out that our unborn son had a craniopharyngioma (a fatal brain tumor) and was given only a five percent chance of survival if he made it to term. After much soul-searching and many, many tears, we made the grueling decision to interrupt my pregnancy to let our son rest in peace. Losing my son changed me in so many ways. I spent many months in a state of shock, depression and denial. It took all that I had in me to get up each day and live my life as normally as possible. I questioned why something this terrible could happen to us – why did we have to lose another baby?

We were given the green light to begin trying to conceive again two months after our son passed. It was hard for me to fathom the fact that, although I was still mentally healing, my body had healed itself. As painful as his death was, I knew that I needed to move on with trying for the family that I so desperately wanted. Part of the grieving process, for me, was doing everything that I could to get myself back to a state of normalcy, and this meant trying to conceive another child. Six months went by, and just when I didn't think I could stand to see another negative pregnancy test, I finally got pregnant.

Looking back, I am glad that it took us six months to conceive again, as this time allowed me to begin healing myself from the inside out. In the beginning, I had been so fixated on getting pregnant again that I didn't take the time to deal with the abundance of emotions I was feeling following my son's death. During the six months between losing him and the conception of our third baby, I learned to accept that his death wasn't intended as a punishment for my husband and me, but a chance for us to grow stronger as a couple.

Hoping that the third time was truly the charm, I cherished each day of my pregnancy and did everything that I could to stay as mentally and physically fit as possible. I am a healthy eater and routine exerciser by nature, and I continued this routine throughout my pregnancy. I sailed through test after test and ultrasound after ultrasound. With the exception of the absence of any weight gain for about three weeks in the middle of my pregnancy and measuring a bit behind at the end, everything was right on track. I was due to have my baby girl on Thanksgiving Day (my favorite holiday) and found it extremely ironic that after all Taylor and I had been through, our daughter was due to arrive on a day set aside specifically for giving thanks.

The day before Thanksgiving, November 25, 2009, I woke up earlier than usual with what I thought was an upset stomach. I was scheduled to have my 40-week appointment that morning, so I decided to just get ready and head out. I had a feeling that I was in labor and determined that the doctor's office was the best place for me to go. The stomach ache got progressively worse as I drove myself to the appointment. By the time I was called into the examining room, I knew that my upset stomach was really labor pains. Two and a half hours later, at 12:30 p.m., my water broke. By then, I was safely at the hospital and ready to meet my little girl. The labor pains really kicked up after my water broke, so I decided to get an epidural. I remember looking up at the clock as the anesthesiologist inserted the needle; it read 1:00 p.m. After two hours of pain-free labor, the nurse informed me that it was time to push. With emotions running higher than I have ever known, I pushed for 20 minutes and welcomed my little girl, Clara Elizabeth (all 6 pounds, 4.5 ounces and 19 inches of her), into the world with open arms at 3:05 p.m. From start to finish, my labor was about eight hours. Although I didn't know it at the time, it was a blessing that Clara came out so easily, as the use of forceps or a vacuum could have been disastrous.

Clara passed all of her tests with flying colors and scored an 8 and a 9 on her APGARs. After spending another hour or so in labor and delivery, it was time to head to our room. I remember how proud I felt as they pushed me through the brightly lit corridors and into the elevator. I was a mother to the perfect little girl cradled snuggly in my arms. Time flew pretty quickly as Clara and I welcomed excited grandparents and aunts into our room. However, in between the many visits that evening, I noticed that Clara was developing a rash. Upon further inspection, I also found a couple of bruises on her back. Thinking that the bruises were a result of the delivery and the rash was just a bunch of freckles, I continued to enjoy the rush of visitors.

Later that night, I decided to send Clara to the nursery so that I could get some rest. She was also throwing up quite a bit of mucus, which I was told was a result of the birth, so I felt most comfortable sending her to a place where she could get the attention she needed. The nurse told me that she would come back around 2 a.m., and Clara and I could practice nursing again. I remember that I had a lot of trouble sleeping that night. I was just so overjoyed with the thought of mothering such a sweet little girl and couldn't wait to see her again. At 2 a.m. on the dot, a woman entered my room, but my baby was not with her. She introduced herself as one of the Neonatal residents and explained to me that my daughter was still in the nursery, as she was under observation because her "rash" had gotten worse. In fact, it wasn't a rash at all, but something called petechiae, which prompted them to draw her blood for a Complete Blood Count (CBC). The CBC showed that Clara's platelet count was 14. At the time, I had no idea how critically low this number actually was; all I knew was that something was wrong with my baby. The doctor told me that they would perform another CBC and would get back to me with the results in a few hours. Two hours later, Clara's platelet count had dropped from 14 to 4. At six o'clock on Thanksgiving morning, just a mere 15 hours after she was born, Clara was admitted to the NICU.

Thanksgiving that year was definitely not a happy one for us. Taylor and I spent the entire day being bounced from doctor to doctor. Because the hospital was running on a skeleton crew due to the holiday, it was nearly impossible for us to get any straight answers. As Clara lay in her little isolette, I sat by her side, sobbing and feeling helpless. Due to her critically low platelet count, Clara was transfused that day with donor platelets. As her counts rose and fell, so did our hopes. What was wrong with our baby? Why couldn't anyone give us a solid answer? At one time, the word leukemia had been used as a possible explanation for Clara's low white blood cell count. What was supposed to have been a day filled with joy, visitors and my mom's delicious pumpkin cake was quickly turning into our worst nightmare. Being the wonderful and resourceful husband that he is, Taylor immediately grabbed my laptop and tried to figure out what was going on with Clara's platelets. In his search, he stumbled upon a disease called Fetal and Neonatal Thrombocytopenia (FNAIT). It seemed to fit Clara's symptoms and explain why her platelets were rising and falling like the late-autumn temperature outside. Thursday passed quickly into Friday. Taylor and I stayed by our new baby girl's side and waited for some answers. The doctors recommended that Clara have an ultrasound of her brain to check for internal hemorrhaging. Thankfully, the ultrasound showed no signs of any bleeding. With the exception of some jaundice and an unexplained low platelet count, Clara was doing fairly well.

I was discharged on Friday, but my baby had to stay behind. I cried as I left the hospital without her. Going home to her empty nursery, bathed in soft pastel rainbow colors and matching decor, and knowing that she was being cared for by doctors and nurses instead of her father and me, just broke my heart. However, I knew that I had to stay strong. Throughout the night, we called the hospital to check on her. Clara's platelet count continued to decrease, so she was transfused with another round of donor platelets. Again, her numbers rose and fell. We spent all day Saturday at her bedside and began to accept our roles as NICU parents. It wasn't until Sunday morning that we finally got some good news: Clara's platelet count was holding steady at 60 – such a glorious number to hear after ones like 4, 14, and 29. We raced to the hospital to visit our daughter, who was now four days old.

Late Sunday night, we dragged our weary selves home for another night without Clara. I think we were starting to get used to our routine of waking each morning, getting ready and heading out for another day in the NICU. Before leaving for the hospital, we learned that Clara's count had risen to 85. We knew that she wasn't out of the woods, but we were happy to hear her numbers were steadily increasing. I remember walking into her NICU room that morning and seeing the message that had been scrawled on her whiteboard: *Today is Monday, November 30, 2009. My platelet count is 85!* After scrubbing in, we headed over to Clara's isolette to take her temperature and change her diaper – two of our NICU responsibilities. As we finished changing her diaper, two of her nurses came in to inform us that, because her platelet count had improved so greatly, we could take Clara home that morning. I was beside myself with joy. Finally, after five days of being a NICU baby, Clara could come home to her Mommy, Daddy and two kitties – Piccadilly and Twinkles. After signing the discharge papers, we packed Clara up and headed home. Before we left the hospital, we had our first family picture taken in front of one of the beautiful

Christmas trees that was on display in the lobby. Sometime in the midst of all the chaos we had experienced, the hospital had put up its Christmas decorations. It was time to go home and celebrate the holidays with our little miracle.

Over the course of the next three weeks, Clara's platelet count continued to rise. A few days before Christmas, we received word that her last CBC showed a platelet count of 385. We could now rest easy knowing that the preliminary diagnosis given to us by the NICU staff – FNAIT – was the most probable explanation for Clara's condition. And in June of 2010, it was confirmed via blood test that I am HPA 1b/1b and Taylor is HPA 1a/1a. We were officially a FNAIT family, and every child that we conceived was going to be affected by this rare condition. The doctor apologized to me as she gave me the news. But, to tell you the truth, I was relieved that we finally had a concrete answer to explain Clara's mysteriously low platelet count.

Today, Clara is a healthy, active, inquisitive, lovable and joyful one-year-old. Each morning and night, I make it a point to tell her how much I love her and how special she is to me. One day in the not-so-distant future, I will sit Clara down and explain to her all we went through to have her and how she fought so hard to survive during the first few days of her life. As this narrative comes to a close, it is important to know that this is not the end of our story, but merely the beginning. This year, Taylor and I plan on adding to our family. We know that our next pregnancy will be even more mentally and physically challenging than anything we have experienced, but we feel that Clara deserves a living brother or sister. Because of our great love for her, we will endure any amount of pain. Only Clara knows the pain she suffered while she was hooked up to IVs and poked countless times for CBCs during the first month of her life. We are thankful for the doctors, nurses and platelet donors who helped save Clara's life. We are thankful that modern medicine will enable us to have another baby. And we are thankful that someone was watching over our baby girl as she safely entered this world. I think I know who that angel was, and to him I'd like to say, "Mommy and Daddy love you and miss you more than you'll ever know..."

Author's Epilogue: The chapter above is the prelude to a blog, which will eventually become a book, that I began in October of 2011. This excerpt was merely the beginning of my long and winding path to motherhood. After learning that all of my future babies would be affected by FNAIT, Taylor and I thoroughly researched the condition before meeting with Dr. James Bussel (a leading FNAIT specialist) in December of 2010 to discuss future pregnancy options and treatment. Although we knew that getting pregnant again would be risky, we desperately wanted Clara to have a sibling. So, in the early summer of 2011, we began our journey down the road to conceiving our fourth pregnancy. On July 10, 2011, I got my BFP (i.e., positive pregnancy test).

My blog, Deep Thought Thursdays, was created to chronicle all of the trials and tribulations that Taylor, Clara and I faced as we prepared for the birth of our second living miracle, Elyse Lillian. Elyse, the product of my first and only treated FNAIT pregnancy, was born on February 24, 2012, after four months of bi-weekly Intravenous Immunoglobulin (IVIG) transfusions, a round of steroids and many months of anguish and worry. Over 13 years later, we are a happy and grateful family of four. I'm excited to share my entire experience with my FNAIT-treated pregnancy in my own solo book – coming to a bookshelf near you sometime soon!

Dorothe Philippe

Mentor in Intuition and Telepathy

https://www.linkedin.com/in/dorothephilippe/
https://facebook.com/dorothe.philippe?locale=fr_FR
https://instagram.com/dorothe.philippe/?hl=fr
https://www.dorothephilippe.com/

Dorothe is a mentor in intuition and telepathy with over twenty years of experience. Originally from Germany and living in France, she is the mother of four grown children and has been a passionate rider since childhood. Her journey began when a healer helped her family avoid a tragic fate and taught her how to access her intuition, an innate ability we all possess. Not long after, she was chosen by Volcano, a young former stunt horse who was difficult to approach. Through him, she learned how becoming more conscious of our thoughts, emotions, actions and language can help us live in alignment, achieve success and lead a joyful life. Dorothe works internationally as a life coach, animal psychologist and healer. She has co-authored several books and is committed to sharing knowledge about intuition and telepathy, empowering others to grow into their true potential.

The Fire Within

By Dorothe Philippe

There has always been an indescribable force deep within me. A powerful energy that animated me. A fire within. It was there when I lived my passion, but also when my mother was told that she had only six months to live. It was there when my father passed away, when my second child survived several life-threatening situations. It stood strong when my youngest got ill and there seemed to be no solutions, when I spiraled into fibromyalgia, when we lost all our money and did not know how to pay our bills. It carried me through when my husband suddenly passed away. It surrounded me lovingly yesterday, when I found my beautiful horse and partner of so many years, having crossed the rainbow bridge as well.

From a young age on, I always felt connected to something greater.

I had the fire within.

I felt strong.

Alive.

Animated by an incredible force.

Lebensfreude – *the joy, the strength, the fire of Life within.*

I trusted Life.

I followed what felt right.

I chose life and the impossible over doubt and fear.

For a long time, I couldn't explain where this strength came from. I was unable to define it. It was just there. I turned to it intuitively to live, to survive, to rise, to thrive, to grow.

Then, in one of my darkest moments, in 2002, I met a healer, I learned about extra-sensory perception (ESP), Chinese Medicine, and I met my horse. All life-changing. Over the years, the intangible became unveiled. The force, the inner knowing received names: intuition, telepathy, ESP, Life Force, Qi, the Matrix, the Field, ancient wisdom, the power of the heart, love, Lebensfreude, this deep, inner sense of vitality, strength, joy and enthusiasm, beauty, presence and meaning. All this is me. The spark. Since then, I have not only been on an incredible journey but also on a mission: sharing as much knowledge as I can about who we really are and what we bear within.

We Are Born Whole

At birth, we are pure potential.

We are love, joy of life, health, abundance, creativity, curiosity, passion, compassion, confidence, trust, inner knowing, the infinite, where everything is possible.

There is no fear.

There is no judgment.

No shame.

No guilt.

No hatred.

There are actually no negative feelings and emotions at all.

They are learned. Passed down over generations by our environment, beliefs, science, culture, trauma, and the way we interpret events and experiences.

As babies, we are designed for greatness. A fetus on the verge of being born forms 250,000 new brain cells per minute, leading to millions of surplus synaptic connections. Our brains then continue creating infinite new neural pathways throughout our lives.[1] Even at old age, our brain can still evolve.

We are designed for expansion and growth.

We are the Infinite.

But we don't know.

You Have All You Need

ESP resumes psychic abilities such as intuition, telepathy, clairvoyance, clairaudience, clairsentience, empathy, remote viewing, precognition, retrocognition, and dreaming, but also the capacity to heal. Every living organism is designed for life, which means that it knows how to find what it needs, how to thrive and to preserve itself. The above-mentioned abilities are not magical gifts for a chosen few, nor are they paranormal. They are inborn and kick in on their own, or you may make use of them deliberately to:

- support and help yourself
- access knowledge and information
- understand events and situations
- find solutions
- make decisions and the right choices
- feel alive and fulfilled
- be healthy and strong
- be comfortable and less stressed out
- create something different and new
- thrive and rise no matter what happens, and keep the fire burning inside.

---

[1] Chopra, Deepak & Tanzi, Rudolph E. (2012) : « Super Brain. ». Harmony Books and (2013) « Le fabuleux pouvoir de votre cerveau. Nous utilisons 5 % de notre potentiel et si nous en exploitons 100 ? ». Guy Trédaniel, Paris : 20 - 21

The Wisdom of the Cell

In his seminar "Touching Biology: Freedom from Cell Programming"[2] held in Vienna on May 24, 2014, world-renowned stem cell biologist, founder of Epigenitics and bestselling author, Dr. Bruce Lipton, Ph.D., shared a fascinating insight:

If you take a cell out of the human body and place it in a petri dish, it reacts to its environment. [3] When exposed to nourishing, life-enhancing information, the cell moves toward it and multiplies. When exposed to toxic, harmful signals, the cell withdraws. If it cannot escape prolonged toxicity, it dies.

This is the key: the cell is coded for Life.

It naturally turns to what makes it thrive and live to its fullest.

But there is more: the cell possesses inner knowing.

It evaluates before acting or reacting. It does not respond blindly. It assesses information about:

- Is this life supporting or not?
- Does this help me to thrive or not?
- Do I need to act or react?
- If yes, how?

To do that, the cell uses intuition and telepathy. It decodes intentions and feels energies. And it draws on its innate intelligence to foster and to preserve its own vitality.

If one human cell can do this, what about you?

---

[2] Lipton, Bruce, Ph.D. (January 1, 2015): "Berührende Biologie - Befreiung aus der Zellprogrammierung. Touching Biology - Freedom from Cell-Programming". DVD. Studio: Neue Weltsicht.

[3] A Petri dish is a shallow, circular, transparent dish with a flat lid that biologists use to hold growth medium in which cells can be cultured. The dish is named after German bacteriologist Julius Richard Petri who invented it.

In the Beginning Is the Void

All ancient traditions and religions teach that in the beginning, there is only the Void.

The Void is the great Nothingness where nothing exists.

No time.

No space.

The void is empty.

Dark.

Silent.

Still.

From there arises a desire.

Springs a wish.

A spark of life to create something new.

Nothingness has nothing to do with the past.

It has nothing to do with what we experienced, nor with what we fear.

Nothingness holds all possibilities.

When nothing exists, all is still ready to create.

Hard times, difficulties, illness, heartbreak, loss, "ground zeroes" are our personal voids. They make us stop, reflect and reconnect with our deepest needs and desires.

Creation springs from what you deeply wish.

This, too, we no longer know.

I Wish

Hafez of Persia, a Sufi poet and sage of the 14th century, wrote:

"I wish ...
For I have learned that every heart will get
what it prays for most."

We do not need to go through tough times to know what we want or need.

As a cell, we know how to thrive.

This, too, is innate.

Wishes, needs and desires are the secret of any creation.

We rise, we grow, we expand when we remember what we really want.

This must not be in hard times.

This can be anytime.

What we think, do, feel and say, then consolidates what we wish to create.

Name the Fear, Claim the Wish

What usually holds us back is fear.

Worries, doubts, concerns, problem-seeing, justifications, timidity – all this is fear.

There is a spiritual saying that all is there to help. So, fear, too, is there to help.

If you take the time to put your fears and what holds you back into words, you will state, amongst other things, that it is the opposite of what you really want.

Name your fears and you become clear.

Claim what you really wish, need and desire.

Then, only focus on that.

If you had a magic stick, what would you ask for?

Be Your Masterpiece

In Japan, there exists a beautiful art, the Art of Kintsugi, or Kinsukuroi, which is the Art of Golden Repair in which lost bits, or broken pieces of pottery, are put together with gold, creating a unique masterpiece.

As we advance on our life's journey, it may seem that we lose parts of our being and our heart.

The life in us, our true nature, however, never changed.

As long as we live, the fire is still burning.

So, look for the things that are your Gold. Nature, animals, sports, art, music, family, friends, like-minded people, your passions – something which represents you most and makes you happy, makes you forget time and your sorrows.

Fuel the fire with creativity, connection, beauty, purpose, love for life.

Smile.

And know:

You are a masterpiece.

You are your Gold.

You have everything you need.

So, free yourself.

Walk through the illusion of death and fear.

Do what you love.

Live.

Your best life ever.

Debra Hillard

Founder of DK Hillard Art, LLC
Artist/Designer/Author

https://www.linkedin.com/in/debra-hillard-93526913/
https://www.facebook.com/dkhillardwraptures/
https://www.instagram.com/dkhillard/
https://www.dkhillard.com
https://www.dkhillardart.com

DK Hillard is a creative visionary, Priestess, and Sacred guide whose work bridges the seen and unseen. With over 20 years of experience as a trainer and life coach, she helped countless individuals transform their lives through physical training. Today, she channels her expertise into the soul realm, using both painting and fabric to create sacred, intention-infused works that invite deep reflection and transformation. As the creator of Soul Wraptures, spellwoven textiles designed to awaken the soul, and Soul Portraits, intuitive paintings that reflect the essence of one's spirit, she offers tools for remembrance and self-discovery. Her work is an invitation to connect with hidden truths, reclaim your power, and embrace your unique path. Through her writing and art, she guides others on a journey of healing, awakening, and personal transformation. Everything she creates is a ritual, a prayer, a reflection — for those walking the path of deep remembering.

Coming Face-To-Face with True Love

By Debra Hillard

In the early days of my awakening, I often heard the term **"self-love."** At the time, given my upbringing and the trauma I carried, it felt irrelevant—almost trivial. My focus wasn't on love; it was on survival. Loving myself was never part of the plan. **Surviving others was.**

Looking at my history, it's easy to understand why. I was raised in a family where persecution ran in our DNA, woven into the very fabric of our lives. When you're under attack from every angle, love doesn't seem to have a place. And when the overwhelming message is that you are unlovable, the idea of loving yourself feels like an impossible leap. Not only impossible, but unattainable. I was continually told that there was nothing worth loving about me, that I was a bad seed and should never have been born. I was told that my life was a burden to others and given the imprint of "unworthy" to carry for the rest of my life. Proving that wrong, paying for my supposed sins, dictated all of my choices for decades. But there was no way to prove this false, because nothing I could do would ever be enough.

Fast-forward through seven more decades of trauma and abuse— and yet, miraculously, it's all gone. How? The full story is too long and winding to tell here, but I can share the key moments that led me to a place of deep self-love and surrender. It was a journey decades in the making—difficult, painful, and necessary. But it became my purpose: to learn to love and honor myself, to **choose life.**

For years, through intensive therapy and spiritual work, I slowly uncovered the path to my own healing. My art became both my compass and my voice. I had been painting most of my life, each piece revealing another layer of my journey—guiding me back to myself. But after a serious car accident in 2000, I found myself at a crossroads, forced into complete surrender. The accident left me unable to use my dominant hand and most of the right side of my body, and the voices of doubt—both past and present—told me I wasn't a "real" artist anyway. After almost twenty years of listening to others, I had nearly abandoned my craft.

And yet, something within me refused to let go.

So, despite the damage to my body, I picked up a paintbrush again—this time with my non-dominant hand. Without control, without expectation, the images that emerged were raw, subconscious, feminine, sensual. They shocked me. I was a bodybuilder—muscular, hardened, conditioned to keep people at a distance. And yet, here was this art pouring out of me, soft and vulnerable, the essence of femininity.

As I sat with each painting, something unexpected happened: **I began to hear messages within them.** Words flowed onto the pages alongside the images, forming a dialogue between my soul and my conscious mind. **Spirit was speaking to me.** My art and writing became my lifeline, my way of navigating a life steeped in trauma and heartbreak. Creative work was saving my soul long before I realized the extent to which it was in peril.

Each new hardship—whether in my health or my relationships—was met with a brushstroke, a written word. It became my way of making sense of the pain, of pulling myself back from the brink of self-destruction. Though I would never have called myself self-destructive at the time, I now see the truth: while my family may have wished me to disappear, it was *I* who had been carrying out their wishes. I had internalized their hatred, believing myself to be unworthy of love. One part of me accepted that lie. Thankfully, my soul did not. I was a survivor, but more than that, I was on a journey back to myself, one that the car accident had greatly accelerated.

Then, one day, I painted something unexpected: a pregnant woman.

It was unlike anything I had ever created before. And then it hit me—
I was preparing to give birth to myself.

That realization gave me the strength to do something I never thought possible: **I left my 27-year abusive marriage.** For decades, I had been convinced—first by my family, then by my husband—that I was incapable of surviving on my own. That I had no value. That I had nothing to offer. But as I approached fifty, I chose to prove those beliefs false. The prophecies that had been given to me over the course of decades from Spirit rang in my head as I gathered myself for one of the biggest steps of my life so far. Far in the distance of my awareness, I knew I was being guided.

This was not the first time I had made a declaration of being. About ten years prior, I had altered the course of my life by declaring who I was in the face of a serious and life-threatening illness. I could do it again now. So, I gathered myself and wrote the words that would carry me on this next leg of my journey. I painted myself right out of my marriage and into a new life. As I did, my health improved. I wrote and painted my way through every demon that had chased me, into the light of a new existence. And then, **I declared myself ready to receive love.** Which meant, at last, **I knew I was worthy of it.**

Now, in my seventh decade, I still face challenges—but this time, not alone. I am loved and supported because I was willing to wake up to who I truly am. Not only have I been able to offer love to another who deeply needed and deserved it, but I have finally allowed myself to **receive** it in return.

But here's the thing: being deeply loved by someone else is one kind of gift. **Coming face-to-face with the one person who needed my love most—myself—was another entirely.**

Seeking love outside ourselves is natural. But **finding ourselves as the true love of our own life is transformative.** I saw it in my own eyes. In the paintings that showed me who I had always been. In the words that had been pouring from me for years. **The truth had always been there—but there was no shortcut.** I had to take the long, winding road back to myself. I had to lose myself completely before I could recognize that everything I had been searching for was already within me. My journey had taken me to the far reaches of my consciousness and back home again.

As a teacher and coach, I've spent years offering guidance to others. And yet, all along, the messages I shared were the very ones I needed to hear myself. My paintings, my poetry, my stories—they had always contained the truth. What had to shift was my **ability to see it.** Not with my eyes, but with my **soul.**

Surrendering the lies, the trauma, and the heartbreak took decades of courage. It is far easier to suffer when suffering is familiar. Seeing the truth and releasing the rest requires developing **new sight.** And that is no easy process. It had been sitting right in front of my eyes all along, but required the journey of a lifetime to see it. Devoting myself to my Shamanic path gave me the new sight I needed to see the truth. Therapy helped, but journeying to the far reaches of my consciousness and connecting with Spirit's guidance profoundly shifted the course of my life and ability to love myself.

I was gifted my creative and intuitive abilities as my way of traveling through this maze of generational trauma. Now, I have developed it to the point where I can use it to help others do the same. Self-love is not for the lightweight among us. If it comes easily, then I have to question its depth and validity. To truly love ourselves, we must see it all, the darkest of the dark, the weakest of the weak, and even the most brilliant light we have within us. Only then can we love, because to love ourselves, we have to love it all. And to love it all, we have to know it all intimately, especially the most painful and seemingly unlovable parts of ourselves. We are, as humans, a complex tapestry of the best and worst of all possibilities. And if we can love it all in ourselves, then it allows us the grace to love it in others.

We are simply mirrors for one another. When you look into your own eyes, you will see both your ugliness and your beauty. The question is: **Which eyes are you looking through, and who are you looking at?**

Loving ourselves is not just an option—it is our **birthright.** It is where all love begins.

Michelle Seguin

CEO of Peaceful Connections

https://www.linkedin.com/in/michelle-seguin-682806203/
https://www.facebook.com/peacefulconnections
https://www.peacefulconnections.ca/
https://www.largerthanlifepublishing.com/

Michelle Seguin is a 'Radical Recovery of Self' and 'Somatic Trauma-Informed' Coach, Speaker, Author, and Publisher who helps adults and teens heal from fibromyalgia, trauma, loss, and chronic pain. She guides clients through self-discovery and healing, helping them find peace and fulfillment by reconnecting mind and body. In 2013, Michelle experienced every parent's worst nightmare when her oldest son, Devin, unexpectedly passed away. Nothing could have prepared her for that depth of pain. Through lived experience and the study of healing modalities, she gained a deep understanding of how trauma impacts emotional and physical health. This opened her heart to helping others. Michelle is an engaging, passionate speaker who draws in her audience with insight into moving beyond trauma and leading a fulfilling life. Her understanding of trauma patterns and their effects allows her to gently guide others to their personal power and confidence through her open, loving presence.

The Queen I Became When I Chose Me Unapologetically

By Michelle Seguin

For a long time, I wasn't aware of what a boundary was.

The word never appeared in my home, during my childhood, or in the relationships I learned to navigate. I lived as if everyone else decided who I needed to be, and I went along with it, unknowingly giving away pieces of myself to people who didn't know how to hold them.

I wasn't just a people pleaser. I was someone who never even considered that my needs mattered. I was a mother, a partner, a fixer, a giver, and an emotional landfill for everyone else's stress. I spent years responding to everyone else's call, ignoring the voice within me that was slowly fading.

I didn't set boundaries; I lived in a world where I allowed others to create them for me.

And my body paid the price. Fibromyalgia became the language my body used to scream the truth I had silenced. I would push myself through the pain, the exhaustion, and the emotional and physical toll of being everything for everyone and nothing for myself. When I didn't listen, the pain would escalate until I found myself in hospital beds, sedated, my body forcing the rest I refused to give myself. I didn't see it then, but I do now: my body had been waving red flags all along. I just kept walking into the storm.

At the time, my self-talk was harsh. No matter how much I accomplished, I never felt like I was enough. I gauged my worth by how much I could endure and by how well I could pretend to be okay when I wasn't. I believed that love meant self-sacrifice, that motherhood meant self-sacrifice, and that being chosen meant shrinking.

Then, I lost my son, Devin.

The pain of his absence cracked my soul wide open. There was no more pretending. There was no more giving what I didn't have. For a while, I tried to live for him. I tried to force joy and fake strength because I believed that's what he would have wanted. But over time, something shifted. The more I began to heal, the more I realized that I had to live for myself. I had to rise for myself.

That marked the beginning.

It didn't happen overnight. My first act of rebellion was saying no and meaning it. No to overextending myself. No to picking up emotional baggage that wasn't mine. Instead of absorbing my son's stress, I started coaching him to carry his own. I began to realize that helping people doesn't mean saving them and that being a good mom doesn't require sacrificing myself.

But with every "no" came discomfort. The guilt. The fear of being called selfish. Some people didn't like the new me. Some were used to having unlimited access to my time, energy, and compassion. When I changed the rules, they called me difficult. Cold. Distant. Some walked away. Others tried to pull me back into the role I used to play, the one that put everyone else's needs ahead of her own.

And I won't lie, I wavered. I stumbled. I questioned whether I was doing the right thing. But once you taste freedom, once you see yourself standing tall, no longer begging to be seen, you can't unsee it. I couldn't go back. Not to the woman who accepted emotional breadcrumbs. Not to the woman who twisted herself into shapes to fit into spaces that were never meant for her.

So, I continued to say no.

And every time I did, I was saying yes to something else:

- Yes to my peace!
- Yes to my energy!
- Yes to my joy!
- Yes to my voice!
- Yes to rest that replenishes my spirit, not rest used as a last resort to escape burnout!
- Yes to healing that runs deep, not just healing that appears good on the surface!

The more I honored myself, the more I began to stand in a different way. I carried myself with a confidence I had never known before. I no longer flinched when someone didn't like my truth. I stopped tolerating being an emotional dumping ground. I made self-care non-negotiable. Daily meditation, journaling, breathwork, and affirmations became my rituals, not for perfection, but for presence.

I immersed myself in deep trauma healing. I sat with my inner child and promised her that she would never be abandoned again. I reminded her that she deserved safety, softness, and boundaries. I told her she no longer needed to carry the weight of proving herself. I allowed her to dance, cry, laugh, and rest, and I provided her the space for her to become whole.

There were days when I wanted to quit. There were moments when setting boundaries made me feel lonelier than I ever had before. However, I learned that temporary loneliness was preferable to a lifetime of self-abandonment. I reminded myself that the people who love you for your truth, not for your usefulness, are the ones worth holding close. And I started to attract those people, slowly but surely.

I stopped walking into rooms, wondering if people would like me. Instead, I began walking into rooms, asking myself if I even wanted to be there. That shift, though subtle, changed everything. I no longer molded myself to make others comfortable. I allowed myself to be seen exactly as I am—no more, no less.

As I grew stronger, the world around me began to change. Some relationships deepened and became more aligned, while others fell apart. The ones that couldn't respect my boundaries? They weren't meant to continue walking with me. That hurt, but it also brought healing.

Because the truth is that not everyone is meant to stay when you rise.

But the ones who are? They will meet you at the altitude of your worth.

With each boundary I set, I became more true to myself. Fully. Unapologetically. I stopped needing to separate the "professional" me from the "personal" me. I was done performing. I was done shapeshifting. I was done managing everyone else's comfort at the cost of my authenticity.

I unlearned the lies I had been taught:

- That being needed is the same as being loved.
- That being silent is the same as being kind.
- That being exhausted is the same as being strong.
- That worthiness must be earned through suffering.

No more.

Now, I live differently. I speak differently. I love differently. And most of all, I *listen* to myself. Not the voice of fear. Not the inner critic. But the voice of my inner wisdom, the one I spent decades ignoring. She's louder now. She's wiser. She's the real me.

What surprised me most was what boundaries gave me access to: joy, clarity, rest, peace, and even *adventure.* I started doing things I had once only dreamed about. I started riding horses again. I played at the park with my granddaughter. I even went skydiving in my 50s.

I wasn't just surviving anymore—I was living Larger Than Life, the way Devin did. I was finally honoring the promise I made to him and myself.

But more than anything, I began to experience a peace that surpassed anything I had known. Not the kind of peace you get from others being happy with you. The type of peace that comes from being in complete alignment with who you are. The type of peace that tucks you in at night and whispers, "You did good, just by being you."

These days, I lead with love, but never at the cost of myself. I trust my voice. I trust my gut. I stand firm in my integrity and let that be my compass. I no longer allow guilt to be the leash that tethers me to patterns I've outgrown. I give myself permission to be misunderstood by those who never took the time to truly know me.

I am no longer available for relationships that require me to betray myself to keep them.

To the woman reading this who is afraid to say no... who feels guilty every time she chooses herself... who has been told she's too much or not enough—*I see you.*

Let me tell you what I wish someone had told me:

You can do this. So can I. And so can you.

Start with one choice. One sacred no. One truth spoken out loud. You are not selfish in protecting your energy. You are not being mean for setting limits. You are not broken for needing space.

You are becoming.

Those old patterns, the ones we were taught as little girls, don't have to be your future. You don't need to be everything for everyone. You just need to be *you*. Authentically. Fiercely. Freely.

And if someone isn't okay with the truest version of you? That's their work, not yours. Find your tribe. Take up space. And stand strong.

Because boundaries don't push people away.

They show you who's willing to walk beside you in truth.

And Queen—you are worth walking with.

Susan Heartlight

Heartlight360.com
Spiritual Director

https://www.linkedin.com/in/susan-heartlight-a287a730/
https://www.facebook.com/groups/1332654857099489/user/1000
00660748017
https://www.instagram.com/nolaheartlight
https://heartlight360.com/

Susan Heartlight, Master Spiritual Healer, is a much sought after expert on counseling; award-winning author of One Power For Good Actions to Create Joy in Your Life! and best-selling author of The Drive to Success High Performance Entrepreneurs. Susan, has been featured on Mike Saunder's Podcast; Influential Entrepreneurs. (MikeSaunders360.com) She started her career in Psychology, in 1992 when she was given the Regents Scholarship from the College of Notre Dame, now referred to as the University of Notre Dame de Namur, in Belmont, California.

Today, when she's not travelling the world or visiting her family, you'll often find her helping people reach for their version of the quality of life they wish to have in private sessions, realizing dreams that fulfill their purpose in life.

RISING: Reality Intuition Spirituality Insight New Greatness

By Susan Heartlight

When you choose to rise in your life, to a new experience of who you are, this begins the creative process leading to the manifestation you wish to accomplish.

The story of a single mother beginning at fifteen years old.

She began in service to others in part due to her natural caring nature and in part to her belief in what she thought she deserved. Her natural caring nature is a constant and natural to who she is. Her belief in what she deserved proved to escalate as she acquired education, skills (fine-tuned by repeated activity) and feedback from others regarding her worth. More importantly, her beliefs were formed by her newfound awareness of her value to herself and her value to others. She cleaned toilets for extra money to feed and clothe her children and herself. She worked in minimum wage jobs, struggling to pay rent. She appeared vulnerable and, at times, subjected herself to relationships that appeared to care and became destructive. Wanting to rise, she prayed for help. People came into her life, and her *reality* began to change.

She thought, "Become more and go to college. Seek a new way to earn income. Earn multiple avenues of income." Her *intuition* shifted and was ignited, engaged and open to receive new information.

Seeking to discover her *spirituality*, she sought out a support system. She experimented with different religions until she discovered one that felt non-judgmental, loving and kind.

Abraham Maslow, an American Psychologist, wrote of Maslow's Hierarchy of Needs. This hierarchy indicates our baseline is food and water, followed by the need to belong. She gained this *insight* while studying in college. Belonging is a need so strong that organizations and gangs depend on this need to initiate people to follow them and may manipulate people to do what they need.

New people come into your life, and choices become *new*. She chose to join activities in college and she chose to become a leader to make changes for others. Her caring nature remained as she chose to fill a need to serve as a leader and raise funds to generate scholarships for people she would never meet. The highest level of giving is to contribute to a benefit, not knowing where or who will benefit.

In time, she felt a stir within herself that was connected, aligned and working with a wonderful energy, the *Greatness,* that is available to all of us. Whatever we place our attention on is alive, and with this greatness, it shows up in our lives, knowing how to take our invisible thoughts and dreams and form them from our imagination.

She continued to learn, grow and elevate herself to seek and accept employment serving others and opened her belief in being remunerated, expanding and building her value and financial security.

She has dreamt and prayed for this **R**eality through her **I**ntuition, birthing her **S**pirituality, gaining **I**nsight, creating a **N**ew life with **G**reatness.

RISING, she reaches out her hands and her voice to lift others and becomes the inspiration. She has discovered the seed within herself and encourages them to find their own seed and grow a garden of living, beautiful, unique, colorful, joyful, kind-hearted women in this world.

Reality: It Is in the Moment

By the time she was twenty-seven years old, she was the single mother of four children and had two failed marriages. Now, at seventy-one years young, she is the award-winning author of her solo book, *One Power For Good Actions To Create Joy In Your Life*! And she is one of the best-selling authors of *The Drive to Success* and an author featured in the anthology, *My Unforgettable Personal Stories That Will Inspire You*. Thoughts have energy and can create a new reality for you!

Intuition Is Our "Red Alert System"

Our "feeling brain" assists us in making decisions. The brain inside our head (hard drive) is our "thinking" solution center, while our mind is our creative/imagination, which is connected to all there is in the Universe (if you will, satellites in outer space). Our intuition may produce a feeling that it is okay to go swimming in the ocean; however, a twinge in our intuition may suggest that it may not be safe.

Spirituality is one of the five dimensions we have as human beings.

1. Spirituality
2. Mind/Thinking
3. Emotions/Feelings
4. Physical/Health
5. Wealth/Production/Contribution

Spirituality is 100% positive and knows how things work for good. Attuning your spirituality focuses your intentions to produce good feeling things in your life. Things like *Happiness*, a feeling I experience when I see a glorious sunrise. *Joy* at the first moment a baby is born into the world. *Trust* when a loved one promises something and keeps their word. Spirituality is aligned with *Creation, Trust, Faith, Love, Hope* and *Connection*. Spirituality is also the part of us that understands the complexities of human existence and processes the sadness felt by loss.

Insight

Seeing into something or someone is available to us when we practice tuning into something or someone. When I focus on you and have a desire to learn what it is you like or do not like, I gain insight into who you are and how you differ from other people. For the most part, this is a fact-based knowing that we can compartmentalize. Imagine it as data entry to be processed when accessed.

New

A simple three-letter word that has infinite possibilities. I step out onto my back deck to see the sunrise in the distance, and with each new day, I am greeted by the sunlit sky or grey overcast sky that cannot be duplicated. It is always new. I walk down my street, and even though the houses appear the same, the grass has grown slightly differently, and perhaps a puddle has collected near the curb, or leaves and branches have fallen. A brown rabbit sits frozen or hops away if I step toward it. I see you in the morning, and your hair has taken on a unique shape from your slumber, and your mood may be solemn or happy. Every moment provides new information for us to take in, process and choose how we want to interpret it. When driving to work, drive down a different street and notice what you see that is new.

Greatness

Greatness is a value that is placed upon something or someone that has increased in appreciation. A greater value has been placed on someone who has become a doctor and is educated regarding the human body, with the knowledge to improve health or to save a life. One doctor may have increased their value by practicing skills in a certain area of the body and increased their appreciation by their kind bedside manner. We each have value in a skill that we can have greatness in. Become the best person you can be, possessing your greatness generated by your repetitive learning.

Speak highly of yourself, for your mouth is close to your ears and you listen twice to what you say.

Look upon yourself and see the light within your eyes that shines the clarity of your heart, brightening by the deeds you choose to demonstrate to yourself and to others.

Feel the air upon your skin and breathe in deeply, refreshing the oxygen carried by your blood to every cell of your body, awakening your mind.

Touch life with gentleness, exchanging energy and generating positive vibrations that ripple out around the globe.

Think good thoughts. Thoughts of love and forgiveness and wisdom. Thoughts of understanding and kindness and great joy for the new moments of each day. I Am Excited About This Day! I do not know what it will bring into my awareness that creates this excitement within me – yet, I am excited to find out!

Listen to one another, fully hearing words and facial expressions and energy. Listen with your Soul, that neutral part of who we are that hopes for greatness in the world. A greatness that gives goosebumps when recognized. Listen for the Truth and risk speaking the Truth out loud.

See through the eyes of Spirituality, God, a Higher Power, Source, the Universe, Nature, Greatness, beyond the physical eye to gain Insight and Intuition and a New Reality.

RISING up individually, we spark another and become the Light of Love, accepting and giving our best. See the unlimited possibilities within our lives and the lives of others. Evolution is constant; we each contribute. Sending love to you all!

Shraddha Chandwadkar

Certified Self Esteem & Brain Health Coach

www.linkedin.com/in/shraddhachandwadkar
https://www.facebook.com/share/16v64Yeg3k/?mibextid=wwXIfr
www.instagram.com/luminouslifelabs
www.shraddhachandwadkar.com
info@shraddhachandwadkar.com

Shraddha Chandwadkar is a certified Self-esteem coach and Dr. Amen certified Brain Health Professional. Her workshops, coaching sessions, focus on practical strategies to improve brain health, boost confidence, overcome self-doubt, increase self- awareness and develop a positive mindset for women and children. Shraddha has coauthored four bestselling anthologies "Becoming an Unstoppable Woman in Health and Wellness Part 2," "Pray Don't Panic," "She Wins Nice Girls Finish First," and "Letters to Him." She is a Reiki Master and a volunteer executive program director at a yoga and wellness non-profit. She received the 'President Volunteer Service Award' in 2024 acknowledging her service. Shraddha is a mother and a spiritual seeker who loves to spend quality time in meditative & contemplative practices. An Engineer by education, Shraddha has an MS, in Computer Engineering, from NC State University USA, and Bachelor in Electronics Engineering from Pune, India.

Rising Strong: How Faith and Perseverance Triumph

By Shraddha Chandwadkar

Welcome to the American Soil

In December 2001, a couple of weeks after my wedding, I landed on American soil at Raleigh–Durham Airport in North Carolina with my dear husband. His cousin picked us up and drove us to her home for dinner. As we stepped inside, my husband "Our home is not so big. It is going to be different!" I smiled. Ours was an arranged marriage, and we'd only spent a few days together in person before tying the knot after a yearlong courtship conducted across continents. The size of our home was the furthest thing from my mind.

After dinner, my cousin-in-law dropped us off at our apartment. The drive was shrouded in darkness, the roads lined with tall trees and deer, and surprisingly few houses. It felt like an enchanted town, a stark contrast to the bustling, noisy, and polluted streets I was accustomed to in India. I was captivated by Morrisville's natural beauty, the graceful deer and towering trees, a scene straight out of a fairy tale. We arrived at my husband's clean, freshly painted rental apartment. Coming to the USA had been a dream, now a reality, and I wondered what the coming years held for me.

Luminous Days

During the initial years of my marriage, I was on a dependent visa that prohibited employment. With a Bachelor's degree in Electronics Engineering from Pune, India, and a desire to remain active, I decided to pursue a master's degree at NC State University, as my husband suggested.

While preparing for the GRE, I enrolled in a few courses at Durham Technical Community College. This not only kept me engaged but also helped me forge new friendships with a diverse group of individuals, some of whom were married immigrants like myself, while others were teenagers. It was enjoyable to be back in an academic environment.

My initial GRE verbal score was not satisfactory, so I opted to retake the exam. Afterward, I applied to the Computer Science master's program at NC State University, but my application was rejected. The department advised me to apply instead to the Computer Engineering program, given my engineering background. I followed their guidance, and a few days later, I received a call from the Computer Engineering department's office staff. I was asked to meet the Head of the department.

As I drove to the university, the song "It's a Sunshine Day" played loudly on the radio, mirroring my hopeful and incredibly happy state of mind.

When I met the Head of the department, he expressed concerns about my GRE score not being the best but offered a chance: a summer course. My only option available that summer was Architecture of Parallel Computers. An "A" was the expectation for fall admission. Despite the course's difficulty, I earned a B. Though I aimed higher, I was genuinely pleased; it affirmed my grasp of the challenging material. Armed with my professor's enthusiastic yes for recommendation, I updated the Head of the department on my performance. To my surprise, I was admitted, and my master's in computer engineering journey began in the fall.

Nausea

A month into my master's program, a wave of intense nausea and dizziness overcame me while I stopped at a traffic light on my way to the university. I pulled over and called my husband. A kind stranger stopped and waited with me until he arrived.

The nausea persisted for days, leading us to a gastroenterologist. He suspected dehydration and a possible viral infection, admitting me for a day of IV fluids. I was also prescribed a month-long liquid diet and suppositories. Despite adhering to the diet, the nausea remained. I began losing significant weight and struggled with insomnia due to an empty stomach.

Tests, including an endoscopy, yielded normal results, and a pregnancy test was negative. However, post-endoscopy, the doctor noted slightly slower stomach and intestine movements. For this, he prescribed Reglan and sleep medication to address nourishment-depleted insomnia.

It started subtly. After my first dose of Reglan, a strange sensation stirred in my mouth, which I initially dismissed. The next day, after a second dose, my tongue began to move on its own, uncontrollably, seemingly trying to escape my mouth. My jaw, too, began opening involuntarily, a terrifying loss of control I later learned was called dystonia.

New to the country and married for barely a year and a half, I had never experienced anything like it. Fear gripped me. My husband rushed me to the urgent care. The doctor there, puzzled by my exaggerated reflex, could not diagnose the problem. A kind woman in the waiting area, seeing my distress, began to pray for me.

The urgent care doctor urged us to go to the ER immediately. The ER was swamped that day, and we endured a six-hour wait. As my jaw painfully opened further, my husband pleaded with passing nurses, but one curtly responded, "She is not going to die! We have heart patients here; we need to take care of them first."

Her words, though harsh, strangely brought a sense of calm. I realized I wasn't in mortal danger and that I would recover. Despite the physical pain and shock, my mind found a measure of peace. While worries of permanent paralysis lingered—*Would my jaw ever return to normal? My tongue?*—I consciously chose not to dwell on them.

Finally, a doctor saw me after six hours of waiting. A shot of Benadryl and some medication were administered, and within 30 minutes, the dystonia subsided.

I was still in shock, but happy that everything was back to normal. I invited my dear friends to stay at our home that night. Looking back, I can't help but chuckle at my somewhat childish reaction. Yet, I'm profoundly grateful for the empathy my friends showed by coming and staying with us. Their presence was incredibly comforting. They never questioned my feelings; instead, they offered hugs and genuine care for my well-being.

The actual issue was nausea, not dystonia, which had been a side effect of the medication. Allergic to Reglan, I could not take it. I had a strong intuition to stop all medications, including sleeping pills, as I suspected they were causing my strange thoughts and feelings. I decided to take control of my health. Instead of a liquid diet, I slowly began eating more, incorporating Ensure Plus to regain lost weight. It took a few months for the nausea to subside naturally. My body was incredibly weak and thin then. I had dropped most of my first-semester master's courses but kept one easy class where I was doing well.

In December that year, during Christmas break, I visited my parents in India and consulted my aunt, a gynecologist. She advised me to take vitamins and gradually resume a regular diet. Slowly but surely, I followed her advice and began to feel normal again. Upon returning to the US, I was able to enroll in a full course load. It took about five months to fully recover, shedding the feelings of malnourishment and weakness.

Internal Shift

The incident shook me to my core, prompting a multi-year search for alternative healing methods. The internet became my guide, leading me to enroll in a Reiki Level 1 certification course. My teacher, an experienced and intuitive hypnotherapist and Reiki Master, helped me understand my overly analytical nature. She encouraged me to quiet my mind and connect with my inner self. As I surrendered my doubts, my learning deepened.

After completing Reiki Level 1, 2, and Master's certification, my teacher suggested attending a body, mind, and spirit expo at the Raleigh Fairgrounds. "It will open you up to a whole new world," she said. I followed her advice.

The expo was a vibrant hub of alternative healing methods, psychics, readers, aura readers, and astrologers. There, I discovered Quantum Touch healing and, intrigued, signed up for the Level 1 course. I continued to practice both Reiki and Quantum touch on friends and family, finding immense joy in these modalities.

My Quantum Touch teachers later stayed with us for a weekend before their flight from the nearby Raleigh–Durham Airport. During their visit, they shared valuable insights on raw food consumption, green juices, and supplements. This inspired us to adopt a mostly raw diet for at least one meal a day, starting with green smoothies for breakfast. That year marked the healthiest period of my life.

Little did I know then that I was embarking on a spiritual path, with each incident guiding me inward. Along the way, I encountered many spiritual masters. Tejguru Sirshree, founder of Tejgyan Foundation, was instrumental in transforming my thought patterns and helping me discover my true self. His system of wisdom continues to guide my emotional and spiritual evolution.

Years later, in 2019, I discovered the path of Kriya Yoga through the Kriya Yoga Institute and the master Paramhansa Prajnanananda. I have found that both practices beautifully complement each other, contributing significantly to my spiritual progress and overall well-being.

A Recurring Theme

In 2011, my family and I moved to the Atlanta suburbs after my husband completed his MBA and changed jobs. The initial years were a whirlwind of settling into our new home and caring for our two young children, then aged one and five.

Between 2014 and 2015, I experienced a perplexing health issue. One morning, after eating bread and milk for breakfast, I felt an intense burning sensation in my abdomen that worsened throughout the day. I tried drinking cumin water, which immediately alleviated the burning. However, I found myself unable to eat many foods, opting for a diet of only boiled vegetables and cooked rice for a week. While this helped me feel better, my weight plummeted from 125 pounds to an alarming pounds.

Concerned, my husband urged me to see a doctor. I consulted a gastroenterologist who performed an endoscopy but found nothing, attributing my symptoms to anxiety. He dismissed my account of the bread and burning sensation. Facing a lack of medical answers for my significant weight loss, I turned to alternative practices. I dedicated myself to meditation, gentle yoga, and affirmations, drawing wisdom from spiritual masters, books, and YouTube videos.

During this time, I also endured unsettling episodes of dizziness, body shaking, and excessive burping, which often struck an hour after meals and lasted for about an hour. These random occurrences, spanning over 2.5 years, were terrifying, especially when they forced me to pull over while driving. Despite trying to eliminate certain foods, the symptoms persisted. Through it all, I continued my meditative, contemplative practices, even learning a few hatha yoga exercises from a friend. These practices were crucial in maintaining a positive mindset and prioritizing my well-being.

It took 2.5 years for the symptoms to completely subside, and over six years to regain the lost weight. Remarkably, my energy levels remained unaffected; I continued with all my household duties and other tasks without issue. The only significant impact was on my driving, due to the unpredictable nature of dizziness and burping.

Triumph Over Adversity

Through these chapters of my life, I have learned some key pointers in navigating life and its challenges. I am sharing them below.

Through these chapters of my life, I have learned some key points in navigating life and its challenges. I am sharing them below.

Embrace Faith and Purpose

1. Have Faith: Cultivate profound faith in a higher power and in yourself. This unwavering belief will empower you to overcome any obstacle.
2. Find Your Purpose and Deep Meaning: Life offers an opportunity to see beyond the superficial. Look for the subtle meanings hidden within doubt, fear, worry, hate, resentment, and jealousy. Every challenging situation holds deeper significance that can guide you closer to your true purpose.

Cultivate Love and Inner Peace

1. Unconditional Love: Embrace loving yourself and others without expectation. This is the true path to happiness.
2. Prayer: Prayer offers solutions to everything. Make it a daily practice to pray for everyone.
3. Meditation: Treat Meditation as a vital form of self-care. Through it, you can understand your authentic Self.

4. Breathwork: Breathing exercises like Kriya Yoga can significantly boost immunity and well-being.

Navigate Challenges with Resilience

1. This, Too, Shall Pass: Every situation is temporary. Do not give power to negative thoughts and emotions. Look at them as passing clouds.
2. Believe in Yourself: You possess the strength to overcome any situation. Challenges are never given unless you have the capacity to handle them.
3. Challenges Are Life's Gifts: Every challenge presents an opportunity for growth emotionally, mentally, financially, and spiritually. Recognize the gifts in every situation.
4. Change Your Narrative: Instead of asking "Why me?", shift your perspective to "How can I make my life and this world a better place?"

Seek Guidance and Learn Continuously

1. Be Aware of Internal Guidance: Trust your inner wisdom; you instinctively know what your body and spirit need.
2. Mentors and Spiritual Masters: Along life's journey, there are guiding lights in the form of mentors, spiritual masters, and coaches. If you find yourself stuck, do not hesitate to seek their help.
3. Continuous Learning: Remain open to learning and absorb like a sponge. Life teaches us lessons every moment; be receptive to them.

Rebirth and Renewal

Life has offered me abundant opportunities for growth and self-improvement. Along the way, many individuals have provided invaluable support, and these experiences have helped me discover profound meaning and purpose. My diverse career path, from computer engineer to patent analyst to real estate entrepreneur, has been rich. However, my deepest fulfillment comes from empowering others through my unique blend of spiritual insights and personal development expertise.

I am thrilled to share that I am now a Dr. Daniel Amen certified Brain Health Professional, complementing my certifications in self-esteem coaching, Reiki, life coaching, and emotional intelligence. My passion lies in giving back to the community by uplifting women, children, and teens through self-esteem coaching, brain health coaching, mindfulness, self-compassion, and self-care.

In addition to this venture, I volunteer as an executive program director at a health and wellness non-profit. My free time is dedicated to meditative and contemplative practices, and I also volunteer with spiritual organizations that resonate deeply with me. I embrace each moment with gratitude and hold a steadfast prayer for a better world for all. My hope is that my life's journey and learnings can offer you a path toward greater ease, hope, faith, and joy.

Agape Garcia

Founder of Confronting Domestic Violence, Inc.

https://www.linkedin.com/in/agarcia247/
https://www.facebook.com/agapegarcia247
https://confrontingdomesticviolence.org

A. Garcia has spent a majority of her life overcoming extreme adversities while raising her two children. With a God fearing heart and purpose driven life, at her own risk she shares her personal story of surviving a double attempted homicide, and is now running a nonprofit; Confronting Domestic Violence, Inc. providing real time resources to real time victims and offering relocation assistance to families that have a safe place to go and not the means to get there. While walking through her own journey of Post Traumatic Growth, she became a Certified High Performance Coach, a 4 time award winning coauthor, Speaker, founder of Be Your Incredible Self and Sr. Consultant specific to Workplace Violence Prevention. Her favorite thought provoking statement is 'You can go anywhere, and reality is, you live in your head! Make sure it's safe and uncluttered.'

Unbreakable Spirit: A Mission to Bring Post-Traumatic Growth to Light

By Agape Garcia

Resilience isn't built in moments of ease—it is forged by adversity. My story is not one of accolades or recognition but of survival and growth. It begins in the quiet of long nights, with adrenaline-fueled mornings scrambling to get out the door on time. As a single mother of two, I discovered survival wasn't just about enduring. It was about transforming trials into life lessons and crafting strength into a daily ritual for me and my children. The journey demanded a fierce yet gentle resolve, protective yet empowering. Amid the confusion and chaos, I found calm—a toolkit for resilience that I now share with others.

My life began in a world marked by distress, chaos, anger, and profound loneliness leaving me with the option to swim or sink. At two years old, my mother left, abandoning my sister and me in a fractured unstable home. By the age of three, I had lost my only sibling, my baby sister, to cancer. Though I was only a toddler, I felt the deep void left by her absence, the absence of my parents, and eventually, the loss of my own childhood.

Left in the care of my grieving father, I quickly learned to fend for myself as he buried his pain in work and escapism. Seeking support, he moved us back to his parents' house. He worked the third shift, partied before and after work, and when he was home, he was sleeping. I'm grateful for the patchwork of aunts and grandparents in my early childhood. Amongst my three aunts, the youngest became like a surrogate mother. She ensured I was fed, had clean clothes, checked my homework, and chaperoned school field trips. She also taught me how to roller skate, ride a bike, and play many card games, which offered a glimpse of childhood. Around fifth grade, my aunts left the house and my grandparents had enough. It was time for my dad to step up and be responsible for the family he created. He did not change his work schedule or life activities. I had no structure, routine, pets, siblings, or cousins. I took neighborhood jobs to earn money by washing cars, delivering newspapers, and mowing lawns—I learned to make my own meals and navigate childhood as best as possible. I became independent by necessity as I was forced to go against the grain with immense responsibility at such a young age.

Looking back, it was the "Survival Instinct" I had as a child. Self-reliance is central to "The Empowerment Check," a personal technique I use today, encouraging individuals to assess their situation and identify what they can control. Prioritizing controlling yourself reinforces empowerment. You must learn where your emotions live in your body to acknowledge when you are being triggered. Where do you experience a physiological change when being triggered? I teach how to identify this, for example: Understanding where your emotions manifest in your body is a powerful tool for self-awareness and emotional management. When you are in tune with yourself, and you apply situational awareness, you are in your most empowered space to respond or react. Once you identify your options, you make a choice, act on it, and follow through. Learning how to intercept your inner critic is crucial, and when applied it can be extremely effective.

School and the recreation park became my refuge because I was escaping home. When I wasn't at the park or school after the bell rang, you could find me doing homework at the cemetery, connecting with my sister- spiritually, praying that she could somehow watch over me and guide me. I remember feeling like that was the only place I truly had an emotional connection, where I could speak freely about how I felt, no matter how crazy, sometimes crying, yelling, sometimes just in silence. I remember one afternoon I got locked inside the cemetery. I had to scale a fence just before dark, running home like my life depended on it. That never happened again, I was so afraid of (I don't know what) the reality of being trapped in a cemetery and the dead visiting me. I had an active mind full of childish imaginations.

It was there in the cemetery, in the silence, where I learned the power of self-reflection, freedom of speech, and a sense of liberation to be a true and raw form of myself to the core. There was no judgment, there was no argument, there were no misunderstandings, it was whatever narrative I created. I realize now, as a little girl I was organically building a "Safety Map,". A process where you look inward, acknowledge your feelings, and map out safe spaces, physically, emotionally, spiritually, and mentally. It's important to have a voice, to express yourself both vulnerably and safely. I teach this now as a means to process trauma to reconnect and align with self.

When I reached eighth grade, I was still washing cars, babysitting, cleaning houses, and working to provide food for myself. I also started hanging out with the neighborhood homies. Little did I know, I was building my street creds. I started feeling independent; mixing that with rage and anger is how my teenage years began. The apartment was barren and silent, feeling like an empty void. It wasn't a home; it was a place to sleep and shower. My father continued working third shift, and for whatever reason, we moved every time the lease expired. With such instability, a true connection between us never formed, no bond whatsoever, we barely saw each other, we didn't talk, no meals were shared at the table, and we were estranged. At that stage of my life, I didn't care anymore. I was bitter, feeling unwanted, unworthy, and alone. Who grows up with two absent parents, no siblings, no cousins, and no one close to share childhood with? The silence at home was so overwhelming, it felt deafening, often bringing me to tears. Desperate for connection, I gravitated toward the only sense of community available, though the choices were painfully limited.

Born to the streets of Chicago, I was exposed to everything most parents would typically shield and protect their children from. For me, fitting in meant earning respect from the streets, and being able to walk anywhere, ride any bus, shop at any mall, which often came at a high price. With drugs and gang violence all around, I learned quickly what not to do, and had to figure out how to hold my own. I knew the rules of most neighborhoods at that point, and knew I was going to have to make decisions. I chose to be a "neutron" (non-gang member) which meant I became a city tagger who ran the train tracks and climbed the billboards to draw art with spray cans - it was literally for my own safety. Those were the only two options to potentially live a longer life. There were plenty of times I was approached on foot or by vehicle asking what I'm about, which meant, which gang am I loyal to. Without fear, I had to look them in the eye without hesitation and clearly state, "I am not affiliated with any corner, I am a tagger, I have cans in my bag." This means, I am not loyal to any gang, I am a street artist and I have my equipment in my backpack. I must take a moment to honor and express gratitude for a neighborhood family who welcomed me with open arms. They fed me, included me in their family functions, let me stay over, and spent meaningful, quality time with me. To this day, 40 years later, they are still my adopted family, and if it were not for them, I would not be the woman I am today. The love we share is real, it is unconditional, it is the only place where I feel a sense of belonging even though I know who my blood relatives are. This family is huge, I'm talking fifty-plus people within a 20-mile radius. The women in this family are true warriors who have endured hardships greater than most people can imagine. Their struggle became a doctrine to our survival skills in the streets. Make no mistake, when I say "in the streets," I'm referring to walking to the store, a bus stop, a friend's house, the library— anywhere. They were very vocal demonstrating many crazy potential scenarios and gave solid advice that worked. As a female, your legs are just as strong if not stronger than the arms of a male.

Amid the turbulence of my teenage years, I found myself in an abusive relationship. I wanted a family so badly, I dropped out of high school and started working full-time. By 18 I was pregnant, which became my purpose and brought extreme willpower. Although I left my partner, the abuse didn't stop, he even kidnapped our daughter while we were outside playing. It was like a movie. He grabbed her, passed her through the window, and took off. I jumped on the hood of the car screaming while he was swerving back and forth until I was thrown off. I had to involve the police to get my daughter back. He eventually left the States, while I continued working toward a healthier future. His mother remained in our lives and manipulated me into believing I couldn't be a good mother because I never had one. The grandmother became so obsessed I had to build the courage to move away and find alternative means of support.

By 27, I thought I'd finally overcome the worst of life's challenges. I was working, my daughter was thriving, and I was attending college pursuing my bachelor's. I was in a relationship at the time, and we were starting a family when he received a job offer out of state, I took a leap of faith and uprooted my life to go with. He moved first while I stayed behind to wait for my daughter's spring vacation, give notice to my job, finish my semester, and take care of other responsibilities. My daughter and I drove across the country knowing our belongings would arrive 2-3 weeks after us.

When our items arrived, I was excited to start nesting. While unpacking and settling in, I found items of another woman. In complete disbelief, I replayed our previous conversations questioning if he had anyone over. My blood was boiling, and my assumptions were running wild. After I put my daughter to sleep, we were in the living room talking, I shared how I found the belongings of another woman and asked him who it belonged to. I was immediately accused of going through his stuff and when I attempted to repeat myself, it turned into a violent attack. Suddenly I was on the floor and he was straddling my 8-month pregnant stomach with his left hand around my neck pinning me to the floor while closed fist punching me with his right hand to the head, repeatedly. When I heard my daughter from the top of the stairs 'mom'... 'mom' her sacred little voice rang so loud in my ears, my brain immediately realized what was going on and how I needed to protect her. Perhaps the words engrained from my warrior women subconsciously registered how our legs are as strong as a man's arms because my feet slammed on the floor, while my neck was used like a kickstand to thrust my hips to the ceiling. This response made him roll forward off of my stomach which allowed me to pop up, run around the couch, grab my little girl's hand as she took the last step off the bottom stair, and run out of the house as we were - barefoot and in pajamas. Banging on a nearby door with lights on, I asked if we could enter and call the police.

The twenty minutes it took for the police to arrive felt like 20 hours. I could not stop crying, it was impossible to make sense of the thoughts running through my head. Not knowing if my baby was safe, I began to question whether I could care for a newborn under these circumstances. I was beyond devastated, shattered, and alone. I was surprised to learn my abuser was still at the apartment when the police knocked. They ended up arresting him and he was chauffeured to a facility with lights, heat, food, a law library, a bed, a deep network, an opportunity to work, wash clothes, have access to a gym and so much more. As for me and my kids, we had the exact opposite.

I was forced into an extreme sense of survival; it was me against all odds. I was due in 45 days, with no option of returning to Chicago. Every fiber of my being and ounce of my energy was solely devoted to survival. I had no friends, no family, no job, nothing. I was at ground zero and needed to figure life out fast. I was determined to do whatever it took to protect my children and if it wasn't for surviving the streets of Chicago as a kid and making it through all that I had already been through, I would not have had the strength to persevere and safeguard my kids the way I was determined to do. I wanted my children to have a real childhood, free from the struggles I endured. Despite my efforts to prevent violence and break the cycle, I found myself repeating those very patterns. This realization only strengthened my determination to change and do better for them.

In the wake of my survival, I stayed off social media, prioritized my family's safety, and focused on providing for my children. The journey of raising my kids would take an entire book all by itself. I underwent several hip surgeries and had major neck surgery from fighting him off of me that night. Learning how emotions can be trapped in your body, I educated myself about Traditional Chinese Medicine (TCM), found practitioners in my area, became certified in multiple modalities and practice numerous techniques daily.

Just a few years ago in 2021, leaving me with a 1% chance of surviving. I couldn't help but question my purpose. As I petitioned God every waking second for answers, day after day while in ICU, one day I had an epiphany: I am meant to share my story. I am meant to offer hope to others and create a framework to help survivors of domestic violence transition from trauma to strength. I became a living testament to Post-Traumatic Growth (PTG), transforming it into my mission to share with others. PTG is a process that goes beyond surviving trauma - it's about learning to thrive in its aftermath.

With this revelation, and after becoming a Certified High Performance Coach, I learned about the 12 pillars of life and how it impacts our thoughts, responses, and energy. Developing healthy habits and staying consistent with routines brings healthy habits and conditioning. What I learned is what I needed to apply to myself. Ultimately, I couldn't get enough. When I renewed my certification, I also founded "Be Your Incredible Self," (BYIS) a coaching business built around the techniques and tools I used to reclaim my life. Each of the BYIS strategies, toolkits, and formulas I offer is rooted in real-life survival, recovery, and doing the healing work personally. I believe these tools are both accessible and adaptable, providing a foundation of clarity, influence, and confidence—a solid platform to build upon and grow from.

My experience as a protector taught me "Time-Bounded Resilience," a technique for achieving goals by evaluating immediate needs and deadlines. This approach creates a sense of urgency, fueling the energy and motivation needed to take decisive action.

The last 18 years of my profession consisted of compliance and audit readiness. In my professional career, I was constantly faced with people in the workplace dealing with some form of domestic violence. Keep in mind that domestic violence is the riskiest call for law enforcement to respond to. For over 15 years, and still to this day, I volunteer for Calegislation, focusing on public safety and privacy, bridging gaps for victims of crime. I'm also a former mayoral appointee, and active member of Infragard, staying on top of current threats from national to local levels while receiving hands-on training from multiple government agencies.

Today, I am dedicating my life to Confronting Domestic Violence, a 501c3 nonprofit providing real-time resources to real-time victims and offering relocation services to families that have a safe place to go but not the means to get there. I hope that no parent will ever have to leave everything behind to escape for safety or face the devastating prospect of homelessness

As part of my PTG work, I ask others to define their lives by their standards, not by the labels or boxes that trauma has placed upon them. I encourage my clients to reflect on the following:

Define Success: What does being successful mean to you? Are you living according to your definition?

Define Spirituality: What anchors you? Your values, your faith, your purpose. Are you living according to your definition?

Define having your SH** Together: What aligns with your core values and gives you space to grow? Are you living according to your definition?

There are proven ways to reshape and redefine the trauma that impacts our lives and experience Post Traumatic Growth. Every ending starts a new beginning. No matter how dark the journey is, every person has the potential within them for growth, healing, and resilience. We each have the power to go against the grain and find peace on the other side. Believe in yourself and stand up for your needs. Reevaluate your personal definitions of success and fulfillment. Remember, consistency builds strength and resilience, and prioritizing self-love is absolutely essential.

Sonya McDonald

Founder and CEO of Sonya McDonald LLC

https://www.linkedin.com/in/sonya-mcdonald-rn-bsn-bcc-7786521b9/
https://www.facebook.com/sonya.mcdonald.96
https://www.instagram.com/sonyamcdonald_/
https://www.sonyamcdonald.com

Sonya McDonald is a much sought-after expert as a Board-Certified Transformational Life Coach, International Best Selling Author, Speaker, and Registered Nurse with 30 years of experience. She received her Board Certification as a LifeCoach from Robbins Madanes Training Institute, the official coach training school of Tony Robbins. She dedicates her life to empowering women to conquer fear, rise above overwhelm, confidently embracing a life of authenticity and fulfillment. Living with Rheumatoid Arthritis and Fibromyalgia for over 16 years, and anxiety since childhood, Sonya proves that chronic and invisible illness does not define you. When she's not spending time with her two beautiful daughters and husband, or walking her dog, Sonya loves ocean sunsets, swimming, and immersing herself in nature. Let her guide you, igniting your inner light and helping you shine brightly, no matter the challenges you face. To learn more about how Sonya can help you, visit www.sonyamcdonald.com.

My Unshakable Love Story: Choosing Me Changed Everything

By Sonya McDonald

There's a moment every woman faces, the moment she stops living for everyone else and decides to come home to herself. That moment was my awakening.

For years, I measured love by how much I gave away. I thought if I just worked harder, served more, smiled through the pain, I'd be enough. But beneath the surface, I was exhausted. I was inflamed, sick, and silently unraveling. I had let Rheumatoid Arthritis and Fibromyalgia shape my days and steal my energy. But the real illness was deeper: I had abandoned myself. And then—something inside of me rose up.

It was the day I looked in the mirror, saw the woman staring back, and whispered, "No more."

That whisper was everything. It was the beginning of the greatest love story I've ever lived, the day I chose me.

It wasn't flashy or dramatic. It didn't happen in a moment of triumph, but in the depths of depletion. But that choice, to stop abandoning myself, was a revolution. A sacred promise.

I was no longer waiting for someone else to fix, save, or validate me.

I was reclaiming the one person I'd always needed: me.

Choosing myself looked like setting boundaries that once terrified me.

I said no when I wanted to. I canceled plans when I needed rest. I stopped explaining my pain or asking for permission to take care of myself.

It felt radical. It felt selfish. But deep down, I knew it was healing.

Because when you live with chronic illness, everyone sees the surface—but only you feel the war inside your body. The fatigue. The pain. The guilt. The grief.

And the only way to win that war is to stop fighting yourself.

I had to stop performing. Stop over-giving. Stop defining myself by how much I could carry.

I was worthy even when I did nothing at all.

And so are you.

Let's talk about you.

If you're reading this and your body is tired. If your heart is heavy and you've forgotten how to put yourself first. If you've ever felt unseen, unworthy, or like your illness has stolen your identity.

I want you to know something: Choosing you is the most unshakable act of love you will ever commit to.

It's not selfish. It's sacred.

It's not weakness. It's wisdom.

And it's not just for the days when you feel strong. It's for the days when your body says no, when your soul feels stretched thin, and when the world expects more than you have to give.

That's when choosing you matters most.

Because the truth is, no one can love you the way you can love yourself.

Only you know what you need. Only you can honor your limits. Only you can decide that you are worthy of peace, rest, joy, and wholeness, just as you are.

When you choose you, everything changes.

You begin to heal, not because life gets easier, but because you get aligned.

You stop living in survival mode and start living on purpose.

You no longer let your diagnosis define your identity.

You become unshakable, not because you're unbreakable, but because you rise anyway.

I now teach this in my coaching. I walk alongside women who are ready to stop betraying themselves and start choosing themselves, on purpose, every day.

In My Energy Intelligence Method, we dive deep into the patterns that keep you stuck, the energy leaks you've normalized, and the beliefs that keep you playing small. We ignite healing from the inside out, with mindset, movement, nourishment, and nervous system restoration.

And it all starts with one decision: I choose me.

That decision changes everything.

It's the boundary that protects your healing.

It's the power that fuels your transformation.

It's the foundation for the life you've always deserved.

You don't have to keep surviving.

You don't have to keep proving.

You don't have to keep earning love that's already yours.

You just have to come home to the truth: You are enough.

You are worthy.

And you are allowed to rest. To rise. To be unshakable.

Choosing you is not a betrayal of others; it's the healing of yourself.

You are not here to be depleted. You are here to shine.

Call to Action:

Are you ready to stop living in burnout and start leading your life from a place of peace, purpose, and power?

I created The Energy Intelligence Method to help women like you reclaim their health, reset their energy, and rewrite their story. You don't need to wait until you're "better" to begin. You just need to say yes to yourself.

Let's walk this together.

Visit www.sonyamcdonald.com to book your free Energy Health Assessment and begin your reset.

You're not broken. You're becoming. And this is your time.

THE UNWAVERING LOVE CODE:

U – Understand your worth is not up for debate.
N – Nourish your body, mind, and soul unapologetically.
S – Set boundaries that protect your energy.
H – Honor your healing pace, not others' expectations.
A – Align with what lights you up.
K – Keep choosing you, even when it's hard.
A – Accept that self-love isn't a destination. It's a daily devotion.
B – Breathe. You're already enough.
L – Let go of guilt. It's not yours to carry.
E – Embrace your unshakable truth: You are the love you've been waiting for.

This isn't just a chapter.

It's a declaration.

Choosing you is the love story that changes everything.

I didn't grow up knowing how to set boundaries.

Like many women, I was taught to be kind, accommodating, and selfless. I interpreted that as: give until you're empty. Serve until you disappear. Smile, even when your soul is begging for rest.

And for years, I did.

I was the strong one. The responsible one. The dependable one. I showed up for everyone, family, friends, colleagues, until the only one I stopped showing up for was me.

But illness has a way of bringing truth to the surface.

It strips away what isn't serving you. It forces you to choose between survival and self-abandonment. It demands honesty.

And that honesty led me here.

I had to face the grief of losing the version of myself that once pushed through everything. The woman who wore hustle like a crown and called depletion normal. I had to grieve her. Then, I had to thank her for surviving. For getting me this far. And then I had to let her go.

The woman I am today isn't defined by how much she can carry.

She is defined by how deeply she can love, starting with herself.

She listens to her body.

She knows when to push and when to pause.

She protects her peace like her life depends on it—because it does.

This version of me is unshakable.

And the best part? She's not unique.

You have this same power within you.

You are allowed to rewrite your story.

You are allowed to create new rules.

You are allowed to love yourself more than your fear of letting people down.

You are allowed to protect your energy without guilt.

You are allowed to be enough, even when you say no.

Every time you choose yourself, you build the life you actually want—not the one others expect.

And that life is worth everything.

So let's do this together.

Let's rise.

Let's reset.

Let's rewrite our love stories, with ourselves at the center.

Because that's not selfish.

That's sacred.

That's unshakable.

I want you to imagine something.

Imagine waking up and not feeling guilt for putting yourself first. Imagine moving through your day without over-explaining your boundaries. Imagine standing in your truth, fully, boldly, and feeling completely at peace with it.

That life isn't a fantasy. It's a decision.

It's the result of one brave, consistent choice: to stop outsourcing your worth.

You are not here to live exhausted, waiting for approval.

You are here to live ignited.

And it starts with you.

So take the first step. Speak to yourself with kindness. Say yes only when it feels aligned. Let go of what drains you. Celebrate what energizes you. And believe—deeply—that you are worth this kind of love.

Your body will thank you.

Your mind will calm.

Your light will return.

Because when you choose yourself, the world around you rises to meet the version of you that no longer abandons her own heart.

That's when everything changes.

That's when you become unshakable.

This is your permission to begin again.

Not tomorrow. Not when it's perfect. Now.

Let your healing be messy. Let your love be loud. Let your truth be non-negotiable.

Because the most important relationship you will ever have is the one you have with yourself.

And when you honor that relationship, you don't just rise—you rise with power, clarity, and peace.

This is your moment.

This is your unshakable love story.

Now go live it.

Janet Hamilton

CEO of The Anomaly Factor

https://www.linkedin.com/in/janet-hamilton-44054323
https://www.facebook.com/janet.hamilton.148
https://www.instagram.com/Janet10hams
http://www.theanomalyfactor.com
https://www.durhamcombustion.com/

Janet Hamilton is a Life Coach, Intuitive Healer, and Highly Sensitive Empath with 20 years of personal development experience. After a long journey of self-discovery, she has found inner peace and connection, realizing her uniqueness as an anomaly. Once feeling disconnected and burdened, Janet has aligned with her soul's purpose and is now living life to the fullest. Having learned the importance of self-love after years of neglecting herself, she became a self-love guru, breaking through limiting beliefs that held her back. Following a period of burnout and introspection, Janet created a podcast and website to share her insights and help others find their own calm and inner peace. Now residing by a serene lake, she enjoys a balanced life, surrounded by nature and supportive, like-minded individuals. Through her coaching business, Janet empowers others to discover their unique anomalies and embrace their authentic selves.

The Power to Rise:
Awakening the Anomaly Within

By Janet Hamilton

What choice do we have other than to rise up! If we are not rising, we are falling. What would you rather do?

Have you ever risen? What does this mean for you?

To me, to rise means to move from one position to a higher one, and to elevate my consciousness and my existence. After all, we are meant to mature in this lifetime, not just grow old.

Rising in love, in health, in wealth, in abundance, in faith, in kindness, in awareness, and all to become the best and highest version of ourselves, to remember who we are, and to rise into being, most of us are doing so unaware.

How does one rise? Well, for me to rise is to become conscious, to awaken to the unknown, and to become aware. Aware of what you might ask? Awareness of ourselves is what allows us to rise into the version of who we were meant to be, before the world conditioned us into being who we are.

We are made of many parts, limiting beliefs, and defense mechanisms that have been encoded in our soma and minds since even before birth, and prior to the age of three. This is ancestral and preverbal, and we carry this with us until we identify them, process them, and release them; this is also what is healing and transformative. We don't know what we don't know until we know it. This is exactly what rising in awareness is.

We also, like I previously stated, have been conditioned by our parents, doctors, grandparents, teachers, friends, society, our experiences, etc., to do and be something other than what we were meant to do and be. Why? Because when we were all little ones, we needed to survive, and by any possible way we could; it is our birthright, not just to survive, but to thrive and this is our responsibility, to awaken to who we were, to understand the events in our lives that made us imposters, how to recognize them, and change them so we don't continuously self-sabotage.

Most people are chasing something—money, a dream, material things, connection, love, etc.—and these are all external aspects of what we think we need or desire. What we need and desire is found in stillness, within. What we are trying to achieve is already a part of who we were meant to be and are; it's our job to remember who that is.

How do we rise? Well, for me, I have been soul- and self-led my entire life. My middle name is resilience. It's learning to respond to life instead of reacting with focused attention, persistence, and determination, not letting anything stand in the way of your dreams and desires. It's dreaming, believing, and achieving the vision that you hold on the screen of your mind; it's all possible. We are limitless in our potential. It's saying yes to me more, prioritizing myself, and doing what I love first and foremost. For me, it is the injustices in life, patriarchy, and power that motivate and empower me to find my voice and speak my authentic truth, knowing that the universe has my back, that I have my back.

My entire life has been led by love and intentions. I have always prioritized the other because I could, I was capable, I understood, and I was fine until I wasn't, which was my massive wake-up call, my complete burnout. It was a message from the universe telling me that I had no choice but to choose myself, and for the very first time, at age 60, now I feel like a six-month-old all over again. I am learning to release responsibility, to find the balance, to rest, and to have fun, so that I can only help those who want to help themselves.

Are you an active participant in your life or a passive one? Are you a victim or a leader? Do you react or respond? Are you intentionally creating the world in which you desire to live, or just passively watching it all pass you by?

I started my own personal development and healing journey at the age of thirty-nine; I was so Type A that I wanted everything figured out by the time I turned forty, which is when most people decide to change. I wanted to have it all in place so I could move on with the rest of my life, and here I am, still at it some twenty years later.

I have always known I was different, an anomaly, longing to belong, never fitting in, never being able to hold and sustain eye contact, disconnected, on the outside looking in. I hear things, my senses are off the charts, I feel things more intensely and deeply, and I have never felt like a victim. I know I am a leader. Now, after going even deeper in the last couple of years, I have uncovered even more layers of conditioning held within me and have learned who I am, why I am the way I am, and I am now changing my beliefs and my perspectives to create the world in which I want to live.

What is a leader? Someone who is not afraid to stand out from the rest, a trailblazer, a change maker, and a legacy maker. A leader is fearless, adaptable, courageous, confident, creative, curious, has a strong sense of purpose, emotionally intelligent, and is surrounded by a community of like-minded individuals who want to support and encourage you to be your authentic and highest version of yourself. A leader is determined, persistent, resourceful, self-reflective, someone who is not afraid to take action, and sets boundaries; they protect their energy and use it wisely. They are independent, self-disciplined, they learn from their failures, they have internal strength, and they inspire others. A leader takes the first step into loving unconditionally. We are all love, we are all meant to be a channel for His peace, we are doing GOD's work, we are co-creating, we are all here because we were meant to be.

Am I where I want to be? Not at all, I always knew that I was meant for more. I am still releasing energy stored within my body that was embedded prior to my memory, recalling what happened or didn't happen to or for me. These are the gifts I previously spoke of, the gifts of trauma, and once again, we do not know what we do not know until we know it. These past experiences and genetics are who and what have made me who I am today. I healed my ancestral trauma prior to healing myself; it is how I eventually connected with myself. Who knew that I was disconnected from myself? My head was attached to my body, and I never even thought about this before. Trauma is not what is done to you, but how you internalize that which was done; this is the disconnection. If we are not aligned within mind, heart, body, and soul, then we are not whole individuals and still have work to do. This journey in life is an individual process, one which only some of us bravely take. Each of us is on our own unique path and journey, and where we are meant to be. We are to be enjoying the journey, the process, the life that we have been given, playing collaboratively in the sandbox of life, loving ourselves, each other, supporting, encouraging, and raising the collective consciousness; after all, we are one, and we are stronger, more effective, and more impactful when we stand together.

As a result of my own transformation and only in the last couple of years, I have become an International Life and Health Coach, an Integrative Holistic Practitioner, an author, a speaker, a mentor, a course creator, and a podcast host. I have created my own podcast, called "The Anomaly Factor!" to show others what is possible when you have a soul and/or mind shift, and that those possibilities are endless.

I have written two books, *Understanding Feelings and Emotions* and *The Caregiver Survival Guide,* and have been in multiple book anthologies alongside other powerful women at She Rises Studios, such as *Beyond the Hurt, The Heart of a Mother, Letters to Him, Becoming an Unstoppable Woman,* and the latest one, *I Rise Up.*

I am also currently working on my own anthology and my own story.

I have a TV episode coming out in the Fall of 2025 with Legacy TV.

My future hopefully entails creating "The Anomaly Factor" magazine, possibly a school, and continuing to connect with like-minded individuals, collaborate, and hold space for others to heal and continue to create and write.

I am learning to relax and have fun. The Lord only knows, I deserve it! It's my turn.

If you are interested in how I healed from Chronic Post Traumatic Stress Disorder and learn how to shift your mind and soul and put an end to self-sabotage, I would love to work with you.

If you would like to schedule a Compassionate Inquiry Session or be coached by me, and/or you have had a soul and/or mind shift and would love to be a guest on my podcast, please reach out to me via my website, www.theanomalyfactor.com, www.theanomalyfactor.ca, or via email at janet@theanomalyfactor.com.

Ph: 1-289-314-0230.

Let me help you find the unique anomaly within you!

JOIN THE MOVEMENT!
#BAUW

Becoming An Unstoppable Woman
With She Rises Studios

She Rises Studios was founded by Hanna Olivas and Adriana Luna Carlos, the mother-daughter duo, in mid-2020 as they saw a need to help empower women worldwide. They are the podcast hosts of the *She Rises Studios Podcast* and Amazon best-selling authors and motivational speakers who travel the world. Hanna and Adriana are the movement creators of #BAUW - Becoming An Unstoppable Woman: The movement has been created to universally impact women of all ages, at whatever stage of life, to overcome insecurities, and adversities, and develop an unstoppable mindset. She Rises Studios educates, celebrates, and empowers women globally.

We Are
SHE RISES STUDIOS
A real-life community of women working to become the best version of themselves to change their lives and make the world a better place.

LEARN MORE

Looking to Join Us in our Next Anthology

or Publish YOUR Own?

She Rises Studios Publishing offers full-service publishing, marketing, book tour, and campaign services. For more information, contact info@sherisesstudios.com

We are always looking for women who want to share their stories and expertise and feature their businesses on our podcasts, in our books, and in our magazines.

SEE WHAT WE DO

OUR PODCAST

OUR BOOKS

OUR SERVICES

Be featured in the Becoming An Unstoppable Woman magazine, published in 13 countries and sold in all major retailers. Get the visibility you need to LEVEL UP in your business!

Have your own TV show streamed across major platforms like Roku TV, Amazon Fire Stick, Apple TV and more!

Learn to leverage your expertise. Build your online presence and grow your audience with FENIX TV.
https://fenixtv.sherisesstudios.com/

Visit www.SheRisesStudios.com to see how YOU can join the #BAUW movement and help your community to achieve the UNSTOPPABLE mindset.

Have you checked out the *She Rises Studios Podcast?*

Find us on all MAJOR platforms: Spotify, IHeartRadio, Apple Podcasts, Google Podcasts, etc.

Looking to become a sponsor or build a partnership?

Email us at info@sherisesstudios.com

SHE RISES
STUDIOS